CHILDREN
OF
THE KOOTENAYS

SHIRLEY D. STAINTON

CHILDREN
OF
THE KOOTENAYS

Memories of Mining Towns

Victoria | Vancouver | Calgary

Heritage House Publishing Company Ltd.
heritagehouse.ca

CATALOGUING INFORMATION AVAILABLE FROM LIBRARY AND ARCHIVES CANADA
978-1-77203-185-0 (pbk)
978-1-77203-186-7 (epub)

Edited by Karla Decker
Cover and interior design by Setareh Ashrafalogholai
Cover photos from Shirley Stainton collection, clockwise: Mom, Ray, and author at Six-Mile Camp, 1927; Meridian Mine, tram terminal, Camborne, ca. 1935; Lodore School, Sheep Creek, ca. 1938
Interior photos from Shirley Stainton collection, unless otherwise indicated

The interior of this book was produced on 100% post-consumer recycled paper, processed chlorine free and printed with vegetable-based inks.

We acknowledge the financial support of the Government of Canada through the Canada Book Fund (CBF) and the Canada Council for the Arts, and the Province of British Columbia through the British Columbia Arts Council and the Book Publishing Tax Credit.

22 21 20 19 18   1 2 3 4 5

Printed in Canada

Captions for page ii, clockwise from top left:
Author's Girl Guides group at Camp Koolaree; Judy Bremner;
Ray Hall, age fourteen, with a pal, Sheep Creek; Jennie Hall and author, 1927;
cousins Carol and Harry Purney visiting Sandon, 1920

Memories for my grandchildren,
great-grandchildren,
and their children's children

WHEN I WAS a little child I talked and felt and thought like a little child. Now that I am a man my childish speech and feeling and thought have no further significance for me. At present we are men looking at puzzling reflections in a mirror. The time will come when we shall see reality whole and face to face! At present all I know is a little fraction of the truth, but the time will come when I shall know it as fully as God now knows me!

1 CORINTHIANS 13:11-12

CONTENTS

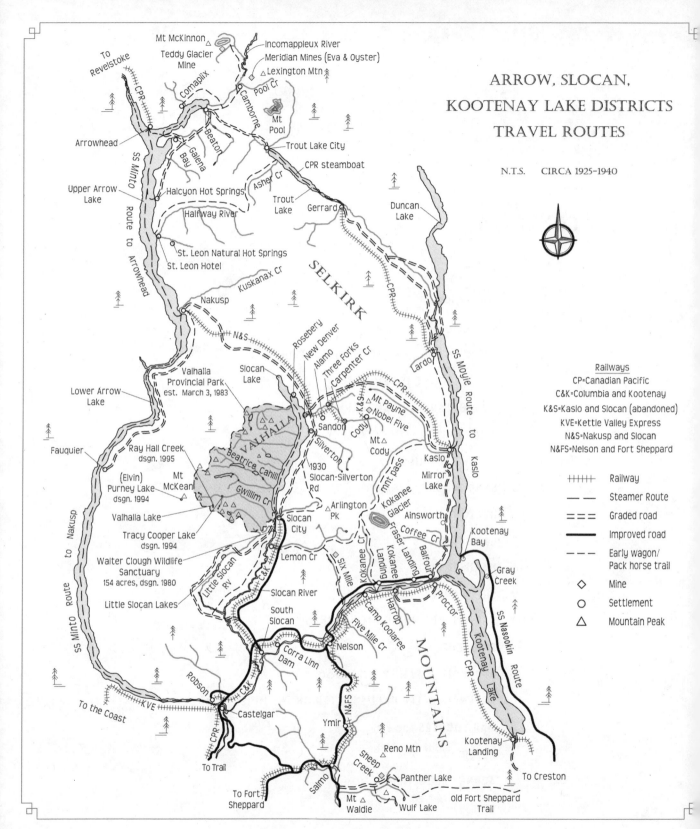

Arrow, Slocan, and Kootenay Lake Districts travel routes, ca. 1930, with the addition of sites named later
to commemorate my ancestors: Ray Hall Creek and Tracy Cooper Lake within Valhalla Provincial Park,
(Elvin) Purney Lake on Mt. McKean, and the Walter Clough Wildlife Sanctuary south of Slocan City.

FOREWORD

DOTTING THE SCENIC travel loops of the West Kootenay area in southeastern British Columbia are the small historic towns, vanishing ghost towns, and abandoned mines that are brought to life through the eyes of my Nana, Shirley Stainton (née Hall). She grew up in the 1930s and '40s in this picturesque area, in the valleys of the Arrow Lakes, Slocan Lake, and Kootenay Lake nestled among the Purcell, Monashee, Selkirk, and Valhalla ranges of the Columbia Mountains. Although it was a time of war and great economic strain, she spoke of a childhood full of innocence and rich with the love of family, living in an area of old growth forests, majestic mountain peaks, pristine lakes and rivers, natural hot springs, and mountain wildflowers.

My ancestors were some of the first pioneers to settle West Kootenay. At first, it was my Granddad who would tell me stories. He and I would wait until Nana had headed off to bed, and then we would close the kitchen doors, make tea and sandwiches, and sit up until the wee hours of the morning. We pored over maps and he told me about our ancestors, his childhood, and the war he fought in. Other times, we discussed life, or how we could build some gadget together, or he would share a secret box of trinkets with me.

After Granddad had passed away in the fall of 2004, Nana and I both missed him deeply. We consoled each other at first by sharing stories about Granddad when I phoned or over a cup of hot chocolate when I visited. These conversations were the humble beginning of this book. Over time, the subject of Nana's stories changed, and short handwritten notes about her childhood memories began to show up on my fax machine. Some stories I had heard before, and many I hadn't, and some took me by complete surprise. I would often phone her and exclaim, "Nana, you did what?"

This exchange went on for many years. The stories pulled me in to her childhood more and more, until I decided to search out some of these places. Nana and I would spread out Granddad's old maps on the table, and she would show me the places where she had lived or draw me a little map of a town as it had been when she lived there. These drawings became treasure maps for me. I would set out early in the day, sometimes with family, to hunt them down. Sometimes we found a ghost town, other times I combed the bushes until I found old collapsing buildings and overgrown water-bogged streets. When Nana could not come because of the difficult terrain, I took her stories with me and read them at the places I found, letting her childhood bring the places to life as I walked the paths. Then I took photos of these treasures to show her later. Often, she would be surprised at what I had found.

In the fall of 2017, I had the great pleasure of taking Nana to see her favourite childhood home in Sandon, ninety years after she had first moved there. That cold afternoon, as we walked, her stories once again brought warmth and life back to that small house and the streets of that ghost town.

KRISTI KIRKELIE

OPPOSITE, TOP LEFT Lee and Mabel Hall, 1895, in pre-Slocan days.

TOP RIGHT Visiting Greenway, Manitoba, in 1939 and meeting
my cousins for the first time. The Shetland pony, Tiny, took us to school.
L–R: Cousin Opal, neighbour, cousin Iris, author, and neighbour.

BOTTOM LEFT Raymond Hall at
sixteen months, Spooner, SK, June 1924.

BOTTOM RIGHT Ray and author, Cody, 1927.

Memories stirred by river's plight

To the Editor:

As the Incompappleau River has been mentioned in the *Nelson Daily News* lately, I thought of sharing a bit of what it was like to live up in Cambourne in it's mining days.

As children, my brother, myself, with our parents, lived in that small community for a few years when the mines were working. Our dad was cooking at the Meridian mine. Mom and we two children were living in one of the old hotels that had been made into apartments for families. I think it was one of the only hotels left standing. I do remember the buildings that were fallen down, were insulated with sawdust and whiskey bottles.

The long evenings of our winters were spent keeping warm with a wood cook stove for heat, and coal oil lamps for lights. Summers were glorious with wild flowers and the heavily treed forests to play in.

Dad would walk down from the mine sometimes after supper to stay overnight, and hike back up in time in the early morning to make the miners their breakfast. My brother Ray loved to help the Brandon brothers, as any ten-year-

> **"**
>
> *The photo of the rockslide in your newspaper brought back memories. I could not help but think of those snowslides. A warning, perhaps?*
>
> **"**

old boy would, to help load up the pack horses for the pack train which took the supplies up to the mine. Other times Mom took us to see Dad for the day. We did not have a school in Cambourne so Mom hired a young school teacher from Revelstoke to teach us for a few months.

The second winter we were there, it snowed so heavily that the road on the Incompappleau River canyon was filled with snow slides. All the men came from the mines and started to shovel the packed snow. The same thing happened from the Beaton end of the slide.

There was only one Caterpillar in the works. It took a whole week to dig us out to have the horses and sleighs back on the road with supplies for our community.

The photograph of the rock slide in your newspaper brought back these memories. I could not help but think about those snow slides. A warning, perhaps?

Shirley (Hall) Stainton
Balfour, B.C.

Letter written by the author on
September 27, 2005, to the *Nelson Daily News*.

PROLOGUE

T HERE COMES A time in every child's life when they become curious about their parents' childhood and youth. I think most parents like to share their memories with their children: it brings them closer together, and sometimes parents have useful things they can teach, especially if their childhoods were adventuresome. So often children never see their parents as ever having been children, only as grownups. These are the reasons I decided to write this book. I wanted my children to remember I was also a kid just like them, and my hope is that through sharing my memories, my life can be a teaching tool for my great-grand-children's children too.

Some years ago, a letter I wrote to the *Nelson Daily News*, commenting on a photo of a rockslide featured in the paper, stirred up other memories. This prompted me to write down more recollections of my childhood in the mining towns of the West Kootenay area of British Columbia. Numerous books have been written about miners and mining town history, but few—if any—have been written about how the kids felt about living in these places. I have to tell you, it was great!

I was born Shirley Doris Hall on February 24, 1927, at Spooner, Saskatchewan.

So, what was I doing, at three months old, living at a mining camp in the mountains of British Columbia? Well, this is my story.

Jennie and Lee Hall's wedding photo,
Alamo Siding, BC, 1917.

FROM THE PRAIRIES
TO THE MOUNTAINS

I N THE WINTER of 1916, my dad, Edmund Lee Hall, of Slocan City, British Columbia, met my mom, Jennie Irena Johnson, of Greenway, Manitoba. The following summer, they married in the now-abandoned small mining town of Alamo, BC. Alamo (or Alamo Siding, as it was sometimes called) was between New Denver and Three Forks, along the Nakusp and Slocan Railway, which terminated at the prosperous mining town of Sandon. Nestled in between Howson Creek, Carpenter Creek, and Idaho Peak, Alamo was built on several benches cut into the heavily forested mountainside and served the mining operations for the Idaho–Alamo Mine and the Queen Bess Mine.

At that time, Dad was twenty-five, and worked for Clarence Cunningham at the "concentrator" in Alamo. This place, however, was a long way from the farmland of Greenway, Manitoba. So how did a man from the mountains meet a lady from the Prairies? Well, at a dance, of course!

Dad was visiting his family in Slocan City one Saturday. There was a dance in town that evening, and Dad remarked to a friend that he had not asked any of the ladies in town to accompany him. His friend suggested that he ask Jennie Johnson, a young lady from the Prairies who was visiting her relatives, the Clough family. The Cloughs lived just outside of town on River Street, across the bridge, on the west side of Slocan Lake in the townsite of West Slocan (lot 61). Dad inquired at the Cloughs, and Jennie said yes. So, they went dancing!

I guess both had a good time that evening, and during the few other occasions they met, because not long after she returned home to Manitoba that spring, Dad wrote Jennie a letter asking her to marry him. Mom wrote back to Dad accepting his proposal and soon caught the CPR

Lee Hall's service photo, with wife, Jennie.
Victoria, BC, 1917. S.B. TAYLOR, PHOTOGRAPHER, VICTORIA

passenger train to Revelstoke to meet him. For three days, she waited alone in Revelstoke where her intended was to meet her, but Dad never came. She thought he must have changed his mind and so prepared for the long journey back to her family in Manitoba.

Just before boarding the train, though, Jennie decided to give him another chance. She sent a message to the telegraph office in Alamo Siding to let Dad know that she had been waiting in Revelstoke for him but was now returning home. Mom later found out that the letter she had sent accepting his proposal and telling him about her anticipated arrival had never reached Dad.

This time, the message was hand-delivered to him. Dad telegraphed her back right away: "Stay there! I'm coming for you."

Oh, Dad! How close you came to causing my non-existence!

Their wedding took place in Alamo on July 27, 1917, with Hugh Archibald Bain, a local minister, officiating. Attending were the minister's wife, Mrs. Bain; the superintendent of the Alamo mine, Mr. Butchart,

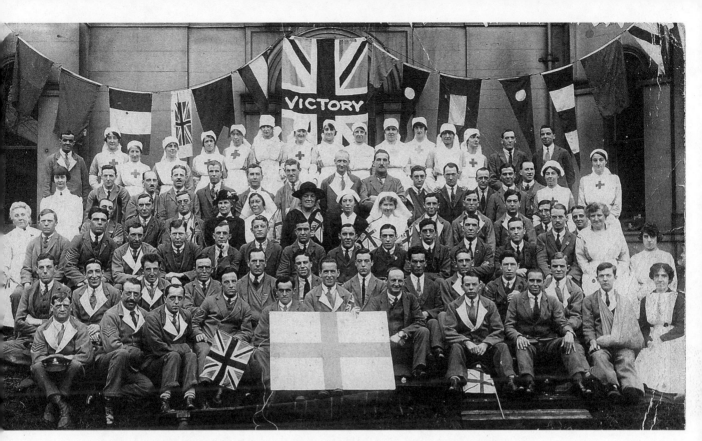

Victory Day, November 1918, Newbury Red Cross and Hospital, 249 Oxford Road, Victoria Park, Manchester, England. The men wore a standard-issue "hospital suit," a blue uniform with a white shirt and a red necktie. PHOTO N115 BY WARD

and his wife; Dad's friends Roderick and Margaret MacMillan; and Dad's younger brother, Hugh Hall. Mom wore a simple white wedding dress with white laced-up boots and a single strand of pearls, and she carried a single pink rose. Dad wore a dark three-piece suit, a white shirt, a dark tie, and black-button boots. They made such a lovely couple!

About two months after my parents were married, Dad was called up to serve in the Canadian Expeditionary Force in the First World War. Canada had already been deploying men and sending supplies overseas for three years by that time.

The mines where Dad worked had been very busy serving the war effort, as they provided the raw materials of silver, zinc, and lead that were needed for tools, arms, and ammunition. But I guess the army was getting short on other resources, such as cooks and soldiers, as well. Before the end of 1917, Mom travelled to Victoria with Dad when he went to report to his post. After she saw him off, Mom then made her way back to her family's farm in Manitoba to await his return.

Dad served with the Seaforth Highlanders of Canada, a light infantry division. It was customary for the men to wear a kilt as part of their regimental and formal dress. (It was also customary to have to walk over a mirror in one's kilt during kilt inspections before going on leave from the armed forces. I never understood whether this was based on some sort of superstition or if it was some kind of parting ceremony, but I was told it was to signify a "true" Highlanders soldier.)

The end of that war came on November 11, 1918 (Armistice Day). While others celebrated the coming of peace, Mom waited for Dad to return, in spite of the telegrams that came saying that he was killed in action. A soldier had found Dad and another soldier unresponsive and turned them both in for dead. In fact, Dad had been shot, but I guess someone else double-checked and decided he was worth saving.

Only one set of dog tags (ID tags) had been found with the men. The tags belonged to Dad but had been mistaken as belonging to the dead soldier instead. Apparently, this is what had created the all of the confusion about Dad's state of being.

Years later, when I heard this story, I asked the inevitable question, "Why weren't you killed, Dad?" He answered that because he was throwing himself into a trench when the bullet hit him, the motion moved his stomach out of the way of the bullet, thus ultimately saving his life. The soldier who reported him as dead later met Dad in the hospital hallway and fainted dead away because he thought he was seeing Dad's ghost.

Four telegrams in all were sent to Mom notifying her of his death, but she never gave up faith that Dad was alive and well and would return home to her.

Dad celebrated the war's end at the Newbury Red Cross and Hospital in Manchester, England, with other recovering soldiers. When he was well enough to travel, he made his way back to Sandon, where he and Mom settled for a year.

In 1919, they had their first home together in Sandon on Sunnyside Bench. Dad worked as a cook. I don't know if he was cooking at the Sovereign Mine for Clarence Cunningham or at the Noble Five cookhouse, but a few hundred men were still working in the Sandon mines at that time, so there were plenty of men to feed. Dad wrote later in a letter that "Sandon was quite a town at that time as it needed a lot of miners, as most miners used hand drills and single jacks [four-pound hammers] to drill holes for blasting, as pneumatic machines had not been perfected at that time."

Sovereign and Noble Five Mines, above Cody Township, 1919.

Jennie, Lee, and Ray Hall, Spooner, Saskatchewan homestead, 1925.

Sandon quickly declined after the war was over, as mineral prices dropped and the mines earned less profit. People started to leave as mining productions slowed down.

In the summer of 1920, Mom and Dad decided to try farming, and so they moved to Spooner, Saskatchewan, close to where Mom's eldest sister, Grace, lived. They used Dad's Soldier Settlement benefit to buy farming property in the Prince Albert region. Spooner was the name of the nearest grain elevator.

My brother Ray was born at the farmhouse on February 5, 1923. At that time, people born on prairie farm homesteads had only latitude and longitude coordinates on their birth certificates rather than place names. Later, these government documents listed the closest town as the designated birthplace. So "Spooner" replaced the string of four double digits on

Mom and Dad's first home, on Sunnyside Bench, at Sandon, 1920.

my and Ray's birth certificates, even though Spooner was no more than a lonely wooden grain elevator sitting by some dusty railroad tracks.

I joined the family four years later. Mom had always wanted a girl (although while I was growing up I'm sure I was a disappointment at times, since I was a bit of a tomboy.) I arrived in a blizzard when the temperature was minus forty degrees Fahrenheit. The family was prepared, though, as a doctor and a nurse were both present at my birth at the farm. Mom had lost two babies prior to me, which may have led to the good medical attention we received when it came time for me to be born. I made my arrival at midnight, so the exact date of my birth has always been in question. Mom said it was before midnight on February 23, but the doctor who registered my birth three days later in town wrote down February 24. He was delayed in returning to town because of the blizzard, which lasted four days. This is why I celebrate my birthday on February 24, and I repeat this story every year, just as Mom told it to me; it was rather important to her and the family.

Our parents must have been planning to sell the farm prior to my birth, for soon after I was born, we were on our way back to good old British Columbia. We left Spooner in April 1927, taking the CPR passenger train to Slocan City when I was barely two months old.

I don't know if it was the rumblings of the Depression that coloured their decision to move back to the mountains or not, but I bet Mom and Dad were grateful many times over that they sold the farm when they did. Dad told me later that he was "not cut out to be a farmer." I guess Mom never complained about the move because she liked BC, and we had lots of family in Slocan Valley, where we were returning.

Detail from *Perry's Mining Map of the Southern District West Kootenay, 1893*. One of the earliest printed maps to focus on the West Kootenay mining regions, it shows rough wagon roads, packhorse trails, railways (those existing and under construction), telegraph lines, towns (some later renamed), mining camps, claims, steamship lines, and known waterways at that time. The map illustrates how inaccessible this part of the country was until the mining fever brought prospectors and the railway.

2

SLOCAN: HOME IS FAMILY

ETWEEN 1927 AND 1939, I knew little about where exactly "home" was: Dad would go where the work was, and we would follow. Home seemed to be wherever we were together as a family, no matter what the conditions were.

When we returned to BC, we stayed with Dad's sister, Mabel Purney, and her family for a short time until Dad rustled up a job at Six-Mile Camp. Mabel and her husband, Alec Purney, lived in Slocan City (located at the south end of Slocan Lake and where the Slocan River begins.) Cousin Ruth, the youngest daughter, was a new baby like me. The Purneys had five other children: Harry, Carol, Elvin, Keith, who was my brother Ray's age, and little Jean, who had sadly passed away on Christmas Eve ten years earlier.

By May 1927, we had travelled up the mountain to Six-Mile Camp for Dad's job, where we would live in a mining camp for the next three months. Finding a job hadn't taken long—Dad knew he could get work with any choice of mining companies in the Kaslo-Slocan area, especially as a cook. A good cook was hard to come by, and the thing hard-rock miners needed the most were good meals.

Although we never owned property on the Slocan Lake or in Little Slocan, the area remained our home base throughout the years. We would go to Clough Ranch, particularly when we were in transition, waiting for Dad's next cooking job at some mining camp. The Cloughs were family on Mom's side. Great-Aunt Ada and Great-Uncle Walter Clough bought the ranch property in Little Slocan in 1920. Little Slocan is the rural settlement that starts on the west side of Slocan River, south of the West Slocan Township, and continues southwest through the small valley of the Little

The author, about five months old, in a baby swing at Six-Mile
Camp, north of Nelson and above Lemon Creek, July 1927.

Slocan River. The Clough Ranch bordered the west side of the Slocan
River, below Gwillim Creek (Goat Creek), just across the river from the
Lingle and Johnson planer mill and the railroad tracks. In 1928, Uncle
Walter also purchased the large island in the Slocan River south of the
ranch, just above Lemon Creek, for trapping muskrats.

Even though the farms throughout the Slocan Valley were small, they
were called "ranches." Most people built their own houses, barns, and
outbuildings, raised their own meat, and grew their own fruits and vegetables. On these ranches lived my dad's parents and several aunts, uncles,
and cousins on both Mom's and Dad's sides of the family.

Great-Aunt Ada and Great-Uncle Walter didn't like to be called old.
So they insisted that I just address them as I would a first aunt. Their
daughter, Phyllis, and her husband, Tracy Cooper, also lived on the Clough

Mom, Ray, and author at Six-Mile Camp, July 1927. The door for the cabin
was a wood panel that Dad pulled into place at night for security
from the woodland animals until we got door hinges.

Clough Ranch at Slocan, ca. 1947. PHOTO DONATED BY
GLEN COOPER TO SLOCAN VALLEY HISTORICAL SOCIETY ARCHIVES

Ranch with their three children, Glen, Innes, and Fern. I was three to four years older than Innes and Fern, and Glen was my age. When I was growing up, Phyllis was like a second mother to me. From winter through spring, Tracy trapped for furs and took care of the family mink farm on the ranch. He and Uncle Wat would travel on the Kettle Valley Railway to sell the furs in Vancouver at the fur auction.

Tracy Cooper came to Little Slocan in 1925. He was one of the first fur trappers along Gwillim Creek, where he had a trapline with Nels Nelson in 1927. When he trapped in the winter he would make use of the various logging cabins along the creek that had been built by the Lingle and Johnson logging company. The logging company also had a sawmill near the creek, about four miles up from the river, to cut the logs into rough lumber before floating the lumber down a high trestle water flume to the planer mill on the east side of the Slocan River.

Tracy's trapline ran from Slocan Lake for a mile or two beyond a cabin he and my brother Ray had built at the north end of Cooper Lake in the Valhalla Range. He took over Nels's share of the trapline in 1930 and worked it for fifty-three years, until he retired in 1982. (Valhalla Provincial Park was designated the following year. "Cooper" Lake, as it was always known by the locals, was officially recognized and recorded as Tracy Cooper Lake on February 28, 1994, by the BC Geographical Names Office.)

Stories about the Clough Ranch alone could fill another book, as the lifestyle there was so different from the mining towns we lived in. I guess my family never went on holidays, because we were always on the move. We probably figured that going to the ranch was our holidays.

The ranch houses and barn were located at the foot of the mountain, above the flood plains of the Slocan River. From the front porch we could watch the steamboats and trains. To reach the river, we would cross over the pasture below the houses into the trees and through a lower pasture.

Getting something to eat on the ranch was also very different. Gardens were difficult to grow at high elevations, so most of our food was brought in by wagon or packhorse. We quickly used up any fresh vegetables, fruit, and meat, as they spoiled fast. Because of the lack of refrigeration, food was usually preserved in jars, tins, or barrels, and meat was often smoked or cured. Even daily fresh milk and eggs were often a luxury for us unless we could purchase them from a nearby neighbour. The ranch, on the other hand, had chickens, cows, fruit trees, and a large vegetable garden— everything one needed to make supper, just outside the front door. I recall one time when Aunt Ada asked, "What do you suggest I make for supper?" Uncle Wat (which is how I pronounced "Walt") said, "How about grouse?" She said, "All right." Then Uncle Wat got his shotgun and said," Come on, Shirley," and we went down by the river and brought home grouse for supper.

Uncle Wat had two cars. One was a black coupé, but the family called it the "coup" for short. It had a rumble seat that I thought was just great. I loved it! One of my favourite joys was to ride in the front seat, where there was only enough room for the driver and one passenger. One morning, I overheard the adults saying that they needed to go to town (Nelson) to get one thing or another; a discussion ensued as to which vehicle would be driven and who would go. I was so excited, I yelled, "Let's take the chicken coop!" Everyone laughed. Well, it was the only "coup" word I knew. I had been under the impression since we had got to the ranch that it was the same "coop," although I admit there was some confusion in my mind. It wasn't that I didn't know what a "coupé" was, it was that I didn't really know what a chicken coop was! I was only seven, and the only chickens I knew were free range. I had heard the words "chicken coop" before but had never seen one. That was my only collision with French. Yes, I was a bit embarrassed, but it was worth it—it got me a trip to Nelson with Uncle Wat in the "coupé."

Walter Clough was an outdoorsman most of his life. Born in 1870, at Perth Road, Ontario, Uncle Wat caught the mining fever and made his way west like Grandpa Hall had, picking buffalo bones off of the Prairies along the way to sell and working any odd job he could do to earn a meal. He arrived at Slocan in 1893 in his early twenties, years before it was a "city," when the only access was by canoe or by hiking a crude trail up the river to reach the outlet of Slocan Lake (see Perry's Mining Map). At that time Slocan consisted of one cabin. Early on, Uncle Wat prospected and mined silver with his older brother, William, and his uncle John Guthrie, who had arrived the following year. As more family followed him to the region from Ontario, he began to homestead. In 1900, Uncle Wat took a job with the Canadian Pacific Railway. A few years later, he married Ada Irena Johnson from Orillia, Ontario, at the Nelson First Presbyterian Church in 1904.

Uncle Wat's job was as a telegraph lineman for the CPR, so the Clough family always had a telegraph or telephone at their house with a connecting line to the CPR station. He installed the first telephone line in Slocan City in 1900, connecting the Arlington mine to the mining office. The first city residence to have a telephone was Dr. Forin's, in 1901, with a connecting line to the drugstore and hospital. Few residences throughout the West Kootenay area had the convenience of a telephone, and the telegraph office was the lifeline for many communities for a good number of years.

Uncle Wat would walk miles of railroad tracks or ply a three-wheel line speeder to inspect and repair breaks in the telegraph lines, poles, and rails. His job was important: it kept the railways safe for the trains to travel on and the communication lines open between the mines, towns, and cities. Because of his job, Uncle Wat had a special gait when he walked based on the spacing of the rail ties. From one tie to the next was too short of a step to take, and two ties were too long, so he developed a gait that was one short step and the next step long. As a young child, I loved to walk behind him while chiming out, "one short step, one step long," while I tried to match the rhythm of his steps. It was really hard for my little legs to keep up and to walk very far with him.

Uncle Wat was a dear, good man. He was kind to us kids and was full of stories about his adventures—and he had lots of them—especially from when he worked for the railway. I enjoyed going with him sometimes on his inspections, and, in later years, on hikes and trips to the hot springs for his health. He worked and travelled on his own much of the time, so I probably did not need to beg too hard to get him to take me along for company.

There was no telegraph-monitoring railway on the Upper Arrow Lake; the area was accessed by sailing from Nakusp right up to Arrowhead and Beaton. Sometimes there would be a break in the line between settlements, so the steamboat would need to drop Uncle Wat off in a rowboat close to shore along the way. He would row to shore, then climb the bank and follow the telegraph line until he found the area that needed repair. When he was done with the repair he would test the line by sending a message to a main telegraph office before rowing back out onto the lake to wait for one of the passing steamboats to pick him up.

The steamboats on Upper Arrow Lake were a branch of the CPR system, so their crews were ordered to keep a lookout for Uncle Wat in his boat and pick him up if there were signs of distress. In fact, there were several times when he was in trouble or caught in a storm, and one of the steamers picked him up. Being with Uncle Wat was always an adventure.

One time, Uncle Wat and I went on the *Minto* up to Halcyon Hot Springs to check the lines. I recall standing on the upper deck of the sternwheeler that day watching it pull up to Halcyon. The wharf was full of activity, passengers bustling about, cargo being unloaded, and shipments being loaded into the cargo holds of the steamboats. There were always many people coming to and going from Halcyon. People would visit from all over. The mineral water from the hot springs was famous for its health benefits and healing claims at that time. It was even bottled at a bottling works building down by the wharf and shipped out by steamboat to be sold in Europe.

Along the way back, after we had checked the lines, we stopped at the hotel to visit General Burnham, or the General, as he was more commonly known. Frederick William Elias Burnham was a brigadier general, medical practitioner and medical author. During the First World War he

Walter and Ada Clough on CPR speeder on the Columbia and Kootenay Railway, 1913. In
the background is the old footbridge from Slocan City to the township of West Slocan.

served across the seas in the Balkans and on the western front as a surgeon and doctor, later continuing his humanitarian service by running
the sanitorium at Halcyon Hotel and Hot Springs. He received many
commendations and medals for his services. I remember him as being a
kindhearted and lively sort of man.

The General had bought the hot springs, hotel, and sanitorium in 1924
and turned the site into an internationally reputable place of tranquility
and healing, a complete turnabout from its former reputation as a luxuri-
ous gambling and party hotel.

Uncle Wat and the General were about the same age. They were good
friends and enjoyed sharing their stories with each other. The General,

Walter Clough on CPR speeder on the Columbia and Kootenay Railway
in Slocan Valley, 1900. PHOTO DONATED BY PHYLLIS COOPER
TO SLOCAN VALLEY HISTORICAL SOCIETY ARCHIVES

especially, loved an audience. While the two of them visited, they would leave me to roam around the place. On this particular occasion, I sat by the hot pool. I remember it then as being a sort of big barn of a hotel with a very large spa-like swimming pool—at least, that was the impression of it in my ten-year-old mind. I remember the very hot water of the springs at their source up on the mountainside: they were *too* hot—you could feel yourself cooking in them. We usually stayed longer at the smaller hot spring at St. Leon. After decades of hard work as a lineman, it eased Uncle Wat to sit in the hot mineral springs.

Another time, Uncle Wat and I drove the coupé up to Nakusp, where he always kept a boat with an outboard motor moored. We were going

View of Halcyon Hotel Hot Springs and Sanitorium from steamboat deck on the Upper Arrow Lake, 1911. The boiler room and bottling works buildings are at the bottom right. ARROW LAKES HISTORICAL SOCIETY ARCHIVES, 2005-024-5

up to St. Leon Hot Springs, not far from Nakusp, in this rowboat-sized launch. I was never very happy to be in an open boat on the water, even as a toddler, so I was nervous when we ran out of gas. I did not mind when we were moving, but I always got anxious when we were just floating and rocking with the waves. Uncle Wat didn't say a thing; he just pulled out the extra can of gas and refilled the tank and we were on our way. You were always confident when you went anywhere with him. When we got to St. Leon, we had to beach the launch because there was no dock for mooring it. We hiked in about two miles to get to the hot springs, which at that time consisted of just a fairly small winding pool surrounded by some carefully placed rocks. The St. Leon Hotel was down by the lake. After our soak in the hot springs, Uncle Wat and I hiked back down to the hotel, sat on the beach and had a bite to eat while we enjoyed the lake view. We watched the ss *Minto* stop offshore as the hotel's small launch darted out from the beach to collect its guests and cargo to bring them ashore.

Mike Grady at one time had owned these hot springs. He had been an early prospector in the region, like Uncle Wat, and they became good friends. Mr. Grady often rode in Uncle Wat's boat to Nakusp when he made his regular calls at St. Leon to check the telegraph lines that ran along the shore.

Michael Grady made claim to the hot springs not long after coming to the area in 1892. He had built some small cottages and bathing facilities around the springs in 1894, in partnership with William Brown, who had built a little boarding cottage at the picturesque sandy beach cove on Upper Arrow Lake. Mr. Brown, a proprietor of Columbia House Hotel in Revelstoke, held the claim to the lakefront property below Mike Grady's hot springs claim. In 1895 they opened the humble accommodations to the public, with dreams of turning the place into a prominent sanitorium, CPR resort, and hotel. The steamboats started making daily stops at the hotel's beach landing by running the sternwheelers ashore and letting down the gangplank. To make communications easier, the CPR brought in the telegraph line and by the end of 1897, made St. Leon an official stop on the steamboat route. The place became quite popular with tourists, especially patrons from Revelstoke. Plans were made to improve the accommodations with a larger, fancier hotel by the lake and to pipe water down from the hot springs source to bathing pools in the new hotel. The plans were delayed; within two years the partners were in dispute over their arrangement and turned to the courts to resolve it.

Mr. Grady eventually built the lovely three-storey hotel on the lake front with lots of amenities, including power, and in 1902 presented it to the surrounding settlements with a late winter grand opening and dance. In the years following, St. Leon Hot Springs gained popularity with vacationers, hosting large local events, and it even operated a post office for many years. His dream to develop the property into a prominent CPR resort hotel, however, was never realized. It was hindered by the constant challenge of keeping the water hot for the hotel pools after its two-mile trip from the source and the lack of either a wharf for easier steamboat portage or road access to the hotel. Mr. Grady closed down the hotel when patronage significantly declined after the start of the First World War, but he continued to live there until a few years before he died. During the war he subdivided the claim by the lake. Several vacation cottages were built, and the area was opened up for vacation tenting. During the years of the Great Depression, the property was often vacant except for Mr. Grady in the big hotel. He sold the hot springs in 1933.

Once, in 1933, our family got together with Great-Aunt Ada, Great-Uncle Wat, Mom's cousins Tracy and Phyllis, and their children Innes, Glen, and Fern, and we all went up to St. Leon, where we stayed in the cottage near the big hotel. It was a little weekend holiday when Dad had some time off between jobs. I remember going there some years before we moved to Sheep Creek, so I was a little younger than I was when Uncle Wat and I would later make our trips, when it was just the two of us.

The sandy beach was huge and stretched way out into the water. The water was so shallow and clear that we were able to walk out into the lake for a long way and still see the bottom. We watched the sternwheeler's crew help the tourists down into little boats to row ashore. The big boats could not make a beach landing at that time because of the big sandbar.

We played around in Uncle Wat's boat and dog paddled in the lake. I loved to play in the water, as long as it did not go over my face. Living in the mining camps up in the mountains, we had no place like the lake. Ray and I had no opportunity to go swimming except when we went to the ranch, and we would sometimes swim in the Slocan River. The most experience I had with swimming as a toddler involved a sand pail, a little red swimsuit with a white lace top, and my mother sitting on a beach watching me play.

For fun one day, we packed a picnic lunch and hiked up the mountain trail to the hot springs. The hot springs weren't much by then. The cabins and bathing facilities Mr. Grady had built years earlier were gone, and all that was left was hot water coming out of the ground, which had naturally pooled in multiple places on the surface. The pools were fairly small; only two of us could comfortably fit our legs and feet into one. In the years to follow, people who went there would do a little hand digging and rock placing each time to make a larger pool.

In the afternoon, the boys also went fishing for trout along a creek below the hot springs, while we girls looked for places to make a fairy garden. The best places were by the creek where one would find a big rock covered in moss and flowers.

One of my favourite times with Uncle Wat was when I was a teenager. He asked me to join him and his granddaughter Fern Cooper to go on

View of St. Leon Hotel and Hot Springs resort from top deck of steamboat, on Upper Arrow Lake, ca. 1929. Note the bear on the beach halfway between the hotel and lake. ARROW LAKES HISTORICAL SOCIETY ARCHIVES, 2014-003-664

a hike to Cahill Lake, which is above Slocan Lake at the Beatrice Creek trailhead in the Valhalla Range of the Selkirk Mountains. After being a lineman for the Canadian Pacific Railway for forty-one years and a resident of Slocan Valley for fifty-four years, Uncle Wat knew the whole area and was very savvy about the surrounding mountain terrain of the Valhalla Range. However, age and some ill health were catching up with him, so the family did not want him hiking alone anymore. This was why he asked us to go with him. We were only too happy to oblige as we loved listening to him reminisce about his adventures and share family stories as we hiked. Uncle Wat was always entertaining.

Beatrice and Cahill Lakes were popular for their excellent fishing. The old-timers said you could bring out two or three hundred fish a day; as many as four fish at a time would chase after a hook. Fishing, however, was not what we were going for on this hike. Uncle Wat wanted to visit his old haunts one more time.

Uncle Wat took us in his motorboat about six miles up Slocan Lake from Slocan City to get to the mouth of Evans/Beatrice Creek Trail. From there we followed the creek another three miles or so to get to Cahill Lake. Cahill is the smaller of the two lakes off of Beatrice Creek. Cahill, like most other mountain lakes, was full of dead brush and logs at its mouth, and of course the cabin we were going to was at the far end of the lake. There was no trail around the lake, but hikers could use a raft tied up at one end to ferry themselves to the other end.

The late Doctor Kamitakahara, a Japanese-Canadian man who was interned with his people at Slocan City during the Second World War, loved to come up here for his rest and recreation. Doctor Kami, to those who knew him, was a dear friend of cousin Fern's family, the Coopers. The good doctor had supplies, blankets, lanterns, etc., stored at the cabin. He came as often as possible for peace and quiet and shared the use of the cabin with others.

On this trip, we planned on staying overnight because Uncle Wat wanted to go on to Beatrice Lake the next morning. We girls were to stay behind at the cabin while he went to the lake on his own. It was faster for him to go alone, and he wanted to feast his eyes one more time on the beauty of Beatrice Lake.

As we settled down that night, he advised us to tie the laces of our running shoes together and use them as our pillows. The cabin was more than likely to be visited by the local pack rats, which would happily deprive us of our shoes to add to their collections. To pack rats, our footwear would be quite a prize. Uncle Wat, however, had used only one of his boots for his pillow that night. So while the rats were trying to confiscate his second boot, the real owner was throwing chunks of firewood at the little thieves as they skittered here and there. This was keeping us all awake. I think they really only wanted his bootlaces.

Pack rats are somewhat larger than mice and are also known as wood-rats. I was never really afraid of pack rats, even when I saw their caches. Nor have I ever heard of anyone being harmed by them. They stayed very much out of sight, and they usually were very humorous to watch. I once saw evidence of their skill in a barn. Some pack rats had stolen some apples and lined them up according to their size entirely around the upper inside frame under the roof.

Fern and I wondered, if there were rats, why were the blankets in the cabin not chewed up? Was it because the wise doctor had hung them from the ceiling of the cabin for their protection? Or maybe the blankets were too heavy to haul away because of the size of the thieves. Whatever the answers to these questions, it is obvious why some of us humans are referred to as pack rats.

In 1980, Innes Cooper, Fern's brother and the grandson of Walter Clough, donated the large island in the Slocan River that Uncle Wat had purchased in 1928 to the Nature Trust of BC, and established a 154-acre nature sanctuary in Uncle Wat's name. It is a fitting location, because it is situated at the base of the beautiful Valhalla mountains that he so dearly loved, and across from the historical Slocan Valley Rail trail which used to be the C&K line that ran from Nelson to Slocan City—the same line on which Uncle Wat maintained the telegraph lines. The Walter Clough Wildlife Area (located north of Lemon Creek and south of Slocan City) is accessible only by canoe and is home to diverse wildlife and waterfowl. From December to March, it is the wintering grounds for the trumpeter and tundra swans and a favourite place for people to watch them before their spring migrations.

Thomas Brenton Hall at eighteen years old, 1882. Travelling photographers would
visit the railway camps and offer their services for people to have a picture taken,
which they could send to family or friends. MORENO AND LOPER, PHOTOGRAPHERS

3

MY PIONEERING GRANDPARENTS WHO SETTLED SLOCAN VALLEY

MOST CHILDREN LIKE to hear about their family history, especially if it is adventurous. Ray and I never got to know our mother's parents in Manitoba, but Grandma and Grandpa Hall lived close by. Grandpa, Thomas Brenton Hall, was born near the sea in New Brunswick in 1864, at a place called Petit-Rocher. He was one of nine children. His dad, also named Thomas, came from a family of shipbuilders in Sheet Harbour, Nova Scotia. Thomas owned a sailing ship and would sail around the world about every two years. He was also the first man to captain a steamship from Sheet Harbour around Cape Horn to Vancouver, BC. My great-grandfather was said to run a "tight ship"—he walked the decks with a Bible in one hand and a belaying pin in the other. I guess that meant when the captain could not control his crew with the holy word of the Bible, he could use his belaying pin. Perhaps this was just a story, but Dad told it to me as the gospel truth! (By the way, a belaying pin is a removable wooden pin in a ship's rail around which ropes could be fastened.)

When Grandpa Hall was about fourteen, his dad took him on board as a cabin boy. They picked up coir (used to make rope) and copra in South America for trade, then continued on around the Cape of Good Hope at the bottom of Africa to do business around the rest of the world. Grandpa Hall told us kids that he saw the image of a ghost ship, the *Flying Dutchman*, as they sailed around the Cape. Whatever it was he saw, Grandpa decided being a seaman was not for him, because he never went sailing again. On the other hand, this experience may be what gave Grandpa his taste for adventure and seeing the world from a different viewpoint, for he

Winch Market, grocery and butcher shop on Hastings Street,
Gastown, Vancouver, ca. 1890. T.B. Hall is second from left.

decided to leave home at about sixteen and work his way to the west coast
of Canada by helping to build the Canadian Pacific Railway.

This was in 1881. Grandpa said one of the things he did while the
CPR crews worked westward was to pick up buffalo bones on the Prairies,
which he then sold for button making. Because he had some education,
he was able to get a position with the clerk of the railway crew keeping
records as a time keeper. He also helped the labour crews (called navvies)
build tunnels and bridges, usually working in camps ahead of the track
laying crews to prepare the land for the railway.

Grandpa said that while working on Rogers Pass, he saw a man shov-
elling black powder from a wheelbarrow into a hole for blasting. Grandpa
said he took one look at him, then turned and ran. By that time, Grandpa
had been working for the CPR for four years and was well aware of the

The Alert Hose Reel Team, Vancouver, BC, set the new world record for the Speed Race in Tacoma, Washington, in 1889. *L-R*: J. Moran, S.H. Ramage, J. Garvin, J.F. McDonald, J.L. McKenzie, R. Rutherford, A. Montgomery, J. Douglas, W. Sanders, T.B. Hall, H.E. Campbell, W.L. Heyward, D.R. Bigger, G. Brown, G. Thomas, T.W. Lillie.

dangers of rock blasting. A good blast would safely break up the rock, but too much powder created an explosion that sent rock flying dangerously into the air, injuring and often killing workers. In this case, Grandpa saw that the man was using too much gunpowder and knew what was about to happen. Sometimes workers would be killed because they could not get out of the blast zone in time. The fuses had to be lit manually, and if the detonation fuse was not long enough, the workers did not have enough time to run to safety before the charge went off. Other times, someone would die checking a fuse because he had mistaken a delayed detonation for a dud, because the charge hadn't gone off in the allotted time. Grandpa said Rogers Pass was one of the most treacherous parts of the railway route he had worked on. Many lives were lost from miscalculated explosions, rock slides, collapsing tunnels, falls from bridge scaffolding, and massive snow-packed avalanches.

On November 7, 1885, when Grandpa Hall was twenty-one, he watched with great joy and a sense of achievement as the last spike was driven in on the Canadian Pacific Railway at Craigellachie, BC. After that, he carried on to the new city of Vancouver, which was chosen as the end of the CPR line on the west coast. Vancouver was just becoming a city when Grandpa arrived, but he could not stay there long because a great fire burned down the whole settlement on June 13, 1886. Vancouver was so new that it had no organized firefighting company yet. While Vancouver was being rebuilt, Grandpa chose to settle in Victoria, where he worked at the H. Ross Co. grocery until 1888, when he moved back to Vancouver and briefly took a sales position at a gent's furnishings and clothier store. In 1889, Grandpa was a butcher at Winch Market on Hastings Street (Gastown). He would hang plucked chickens, tuna, and butchered meat upside down out in the "fresh air" right in the storefront; he told us that as a butcher in those days, it was a perfectly natural thing to do. He worked in Vancouver as a grocer/butcher from 1889 to 1896, when at some point he owned his own market, called Beatty and Hall, on Cordova Street. In 1897, he moved his family to Victoria, where they lived for a little over a year while he partnered with Ross Co. and made plans to move his family to Slocan Valley.

Grandpa also became a firefighter for the Vancouver Volunteer Fire Brigade and competed on the Alert Hose Reel Team of Vancouver. I wonder if the Great Vancouver Fire of 1886 had anything to do with his deciding to join the brigade.

I don't know the story of how my Hall grandparents met. I believe they most likely met sometime around or after the Great Seattle Fire of June 1889. The fire was so immense that the city called for fire brigades to come and help fight it from as far away as Victoria and Vancouver. Grandpa could have met Grandma Hall during his trip to that area as a member of the fire brigade, or when he was competing on the Alert Hose Reel Team in Tacoma a few months later. Tacoma held a four-day International Fire Tournament in September 1889. The Vancouver Alert Hose Reel Team entered all four races in the tournament and placed in all four. The team won first place in the Dry Test Hose Race and the Speed Race, and placed second in the Wet Test Hose Race and the Championship Race. They set a new world record for the Speed Race and beat out the twelve other teams to win the overall team championship red ribbon. Each member of the Vancouver team also received a gold-plated medallion with his name engraved on the back. Grandpa's medallion reads "Tacoma, T.B. Hall, 1889."

Grandma Hall (née Carrie Maria Carr) was born October 5, 1864, the same birth year as Grandpa. I was told that she was born at the blockhouse called Fort Decatur in Seattle. We always celebrated my grandparents' birthdays together, as they claimed that they were born on the same day, even though census records show that Thomas was born on October 7. The records also show Thomas was born in Bathurst, instead of Petite Rocher, but from personal experience, I've found that historical government records are not always accurate (my birth record being case in point). Or perhaps the records are true, and Grandma and Grandpa just decided to split the difference like good couples often do in such matters. Either way we always had the best of times celebrating with them.

My grandparent's courtship was a short one, about three months by my estimation. Carrie visited Thomas in Vancouver that winter and she married him there on

The medal and red first place winners ribbon pinned on the Alert Hose Reel Team's shirts.

Carrie Maria Carr, Tacoma, Washington, ca. 1889.

December 14, 1889, with the blessings of her siblings still in Seattle. Her younger sister, Abbie (Carr), had made the trip with her and was Carrie's witness at the wedding. The minister's wife was the only other guest. Carrie's mother, father, and grandmother had all passed away a few years prior to her meeting Grandpa Hall.

Carrie Carr was one of the daughters of Edmund Carr, an early settler of Seattle. Edmund was also a great traveller, as I understand it; he had travelled the Oregon Trail three times as a guide. He was born May 5, 1824, at the small seaport town of Bucksport, Maine, and came to Seattle in early February of 1853 via the Isthmus of Panama, with his brother. He then settled a donation land claim (164.98 acres) of three adjoining lots on the south side of Salmon Bay, which adjoined the north boundary of Dr. Henry Smith's claim of the cove. Edmund and Dr. Smith were two of the earliest pioneers to settle the area now known as Interbay.

During the Puget Sound War of 1855–56, Great-Grandpa Carr volunteered to protect the settlers against a group of hostile Native people as the settlers fled their claims for the safety of the blockhouses. The north blockhouse was named Fort Decatur after the USS *Decatur*, which was anchored in Elliot Bay. The *Decatur*'s crew had used the ship's artillery fire to drive off the attackers and sent marines to the aid of the settlers. Fort Decatur was situated on a knoll overlooking Yesler's mill and wharf. In modern-day Seattle, it was on the corner where First Avenue and Cherry Street intersect, across from Pioneer Square Park.

Although Edmund had stood with the settlers against the hostilities of the Native people, he was good friends with Chief Seattle, who had kept the peace between the majority of the local tribes and the settlers. Grandma Carrie Hall told my dad that Chief Seattle's daughter, Angeline, would babysit them. Grandma Hall described her as a gentle, sweet, kind person.

Edmund Carr married Olivia Holgate on June 5, 1856; she was from one of the settler families he had protected at the fort. Her youngest brother, Milton, was not as lucky, as he was killed by Native fire just before reaching the safety of the blockhouse on the morning of the Battle of Seattle, January 26, 1856. He was fifteen years old. Olivia was one of Elizabeth Holgate's nine children, five of whom had left their homestead with their mother, along with many other pioneers from Van Buren, Iowa, to start a new life in the Washington Territory. Grandma Hall would tell me the story, while she treated me to milk and cookies, of how her mother had carefully packed the few precious possessions that they could bring, and then travelled for many months by covered wagon pulled by oxen over the dusty, bumpy, very long, and sometimes dangerous Oregon Trail.

The Holgates first heard about Seattle from Elizabeth's son John Cornelius Holgate, who had left the Iowa family homestead in early 1847 and travelled west on the Oregon Trail looking for a new place to settle—and for someone to marry. He finally reached the Pacific coast by the summer of 1850 and came upon the area of future Seattle while exploring Puget Sound by canoe. He wrote to his family about its beautiful forests and bountiful food, trying to convince them to emigrate, but the family would not leave their homestead, despite his father (Abraham) having died in a blizzard some years earlier. Three years later, the Holgates finally decided to make the move to Seattle and sent word to John. John staked a 320-acre script claim in 1853 to get ready for the family's arrival. After they arrived, Edward and Abigail (née Holgate) Hanford also staked a 320-acre claim adjoining the south boundary of John's claim in January 1854, while brother Lemuel Holgate, staked 161.81 acres adjoining Edward's east boundary. This block of Holgate claims is now known as the Beacon Hill and Mount Baker areas in modern Seattle, and the only hint of its previous owners is the street named South Holgate, which follows the northern-most boundary line of the claims. Lemuel also made another land claim on the north side of Salmon Bay across from Edmund Carr's claim. Elizabeth Holgate lived at the house on Cherry Street, on the north side of Cherry Street midway between Second and Third Avenues, about half a block away from Fort Decatur. When it was spoiled during the Battle of Seattle, she lived with her sons on their properties.

In 1857, Great-Grandpa Carr left his claim to take a position as a probate judge in Port Townsend. In 1861, he and two other men, Daniel Bagley and John Webster, were appointed commissioners to establish the Territorial University of Washington. Great-Grandpa Carr served on the first board of regents of the University of Washington and was involved in overseeing the growth of public schools in King County from 1861 to 1875. He was the county superintendent of schools from 1863 to 1872.

After he retired from the board, Edmund Carr became a fulltime farmer. Dad said that Great-Grandpa was responsible for the successful propagation of the white potato in the region. The potatoes in the area had developed some kind of scab disease, so Edmund asked his relatives in Maine to send him a few potato sprouts, which he planted and cultivated. The variety was called Peach Bloom; it had a better resistance to the scab. Over many years, he shared the potatoes he cultivated with others until the variety was widely grown all over the territory. Great-Grandpa Carr died in Seattle on November 16, 1886. I was told that Great-Grandma Olivia died in 1881 of typhoid fever, likely caught while nursing patients suffering from the disease.

I have to add a little account here about Dad's uncle Ullie (Ulrich) Carr, who was a suit salesman at the logging camps around Seattle. He married a lady who, the family was told, was a granddaughter of William Clark, of the famed explorers Lewis and Clark who explored the northwestern part of the US for the federal government from 1804 to 1806. I never found evidence to substantiate the claim, but then again, Auntie had no reason to lie. True or not, the family, including Dad, Ray, and me, loved to refer to Aunt Etta by her full name, which was Henrietta Anna May Eclipse Clark Reid Carr. "Eclipse" came from the fact she was born during an eclipse of the moon; "Clark" was her surname; "Reid" was her last name from her first marriage (she had been widowed); and "Carr," of course, was Uncle Ullie's surname. Aunt Etta's full name was one I would never forget.

Many of these stories were told to me by Dad. I asked him why Grandma Hall had told them just to him. His answer was, "I was a sickly child and at home a lot. That was when she entertained me with her childhood and family history." As an adult, I spent time in Seattle checking into the family history and Grandma's stories that she had told Dad. I found many things that bore them out.

After Grandpa and Grandma Hall got married, they first settled in Vancouver, where they had three children. Aunt Mabel was the oldest, Uncle Hugh the youngest, and Dad was the middle child. My dad, Edmund Lee Hall, was registered as the twenty-fifth baby to be born in Vancouver. Of course, more than twenty-five children had been born in Vancouver before him, but Dad was the twenty-fifth to be issued a birth certificate. Some years later, Dad wrote to the registrar's office for a copy of his birth certificate. The person who sent it included a note saying that he was the man who had originally registered Dad's birth. Dad got a kick out of that!

I did not know my dad's siblings all that well. When I was about six both Aunt Mabel and her husband, Uncle Alec, got very sick and died within the next three years. Aunt Mabel passed away first, in 1934, then Uncle Alec two years later, leaving their five children behind. My cousin Ruth was about seven when she went to live with our grandparents in Nelson, after they had built their new house there in Fairview (a district of Nelson). I'm not sure where the boys, Elvin, Keith, and Harry, went at that time, but their sister Carol began training as a nurse in the Nelson Hospital after she had spent the last two years nursing her sick father. Keith and Harry both visited Mom, Dad, and me at our home in Nelson in later years. Both Ruth and Carol died in automobile accidents later in life, and Elvin was shot down while flying over Belgium during the Second World War. On November 10, 1994, the BC Ministry of Environment, Lands and Parks honoured my cousin, Private Officer Elvin C. Purney, in the BC Remembrance Day list of geographical names, by naming a small lake west of the Valhalla Provincial Park, above Slocan Lake, Purney Lake.

Uncle Hugh, Dad's brother, married into our American side. He and his cousin, Aunt Bertha, and their children have always lived in the United States in and around Edmonds, Washington.

View of the stables at Thomas Brenton Hall Ranch, Little Slocan, 1900.

Around the summer of 1898, the Halls moved from Victoria to Little Slocan, and bought property from the Larson family in the Robinson (Mulvey) Creek Valley, not far from Slocan City. They built their first home there. I guess Grandpa's fiddle foot just took him there, probably after hearing about the mines and jobs in that area. Because Grandma Hall was a pioneer from Seattle, pioneering living conditions were something she was accustomed to. Dad did tell me that Grandpa Hall once mentioned travelling up to Alaska during the gold rush, but Grandma said, "You've got me this far north and I am not going any farther!"

DAD, MABEL, AND Hugh were all schooled in Slocan City in the early 1900s. Dad told the story of one of his school days in Slocan. The older boys had heard that the steamboat *Hunter* was loaded with Chinese workers coming down the lake to do some work in Slocan City and that the townsmen would not let them land. I think it had something to do with the miners' union. The townspeople also had a great deal of fear that the

Pupils at Slocan City School, 1899. *L–R. Back row (names from back of photo):* Archie Bunting, Lee Hall, Ed Tiffing, Gus Balks, Alex McCallum, Herman Lindors, Ernnett Tutcher, Fred York, Pat Foley. *Fourth row:* Gertrude York, Chas Tiffing, Frank Benish, Mildred Lavell, Mary Benish, Mabel Hall, Francis Tutcher, William Smith, Miss Moss. *Third row:* B. Smith, Wes Baty, Rosslea Smith, Julia Madigan. *Second row:* Adolph Beck, Nettie Bull, Remelard, Wichman, Annie Rae Wichman, Hugh Hall, Baty, Jan Robertson, Foley, Alice Bull. *Front row:* Lorne Foley, Wichman, Remelard, Lizzie Rae, Lavell, Harris Ross, Foley.

Chinese immigrants, who would work for less money, would take jobs away from the people who were already settled in the area. Dad's teacher, Mr. Hindle, told the boys that if they went to the dock to see the sight, they would get a "licking" (presumably a paddling) when they came back. Dad said they went anyway. And when they returned, they got their lickings.

Another school story was about when Grandpa took the family down to California to visit some relatives in 1902. It was an extended stay, so the children were attending the school in the area they were visiting. The teacher told the children that Canada was a land of ice and snow. Well, that did not sit well with young Hugh, who told the teacher she was wrong. Hugh was chastised by her, but the teacher was even more shocked

Lee Hall with a small team of horses ploughing the field
at the ranch in Little Slocan, 1913. Dad is twenty-one.

when Grandpa Hall told her that it was the truth, and the textbook was wrong.

Dad said that they also had the chance to see Buffalo Bill's Wild West show on this visit to California. He was ten years old.

Dad attended school until he was fourteen, at which time Grandpa took him out of school so he could help him with a cooking job at the Arlington mine. Where Grandpa learned to cook, I do not know, but it could have been as a cabin boy on his father's ship. I don't believe Dad ever returned to his studies.

Grandpa Hall was already leaving a cooking position at the Ottawa mine, and took the new job at the Arlington mine at the request of a telegram from W.F. DuBois in December 1906. Apparently, Mr. DuBois had been wanting Grandpa to come and cook for the Arlington and bake bread for his family for some time. Dad was to work as an ore sorter, do chores, and be his dad's flunky for ten hours each day. Dad learned to cook from Grandpa. By age eighteen, Dad was cooking at mines—first the Ottawa, then the Enterprise. He also hauled ore from the Enterprise mine, first "raw-hiding" the load across deep snow with horses that wore snowshoes, then hauling it the next day by wagon with a different team of horses down to the landing at Ten Mile Bay. The ore was then shipped to the mill by barge and steamboat. By 1913, when he was twenty-one, he was cooking at the Surprise Mine, near Sandon.

In 1917, Dad worked for a man named Clarence Cunningham, driving a four-horse team that pulled an ore wagon from the Queen Bess Mine nine miles down to Sandon. From there, the ore was put on railcars and shipped first for processing to the old concentrator at Alamo Siding and then to the Cominco Smelter in Trail, BC, which was owned by CPR at that time. His pay was $150 a month. This was big money at that time. (This was before Mr. Cunningham replaced the old mill at Alamo Siding with a new, water-powered, all-fine crushing mill and connected the Queen Bess and Idaho-Alamo mines to the mill with aerial tramways to haul ore buckets.)

Dad had a fantastic memory for names and events, even as a child. One such event was the last public hanging in Nelson, of a man named Henry Rose who was found guilty of the brutal murder of his business partner, John Cole. A heritage marker now stands where Mr. Rose had his log cabin at the north end of Gray Creek. The cabin is gone, but the story of why he was hanged is recorded on this marker. The hanging took place in Nelson in November 1902. I don't remember whether Dad was alone when he saw it, or if someone brought him there, but for some reason he was there and watched the hanging. He was only ten years old. Dad never said how he felt, but I guess it left quite an impression on him, because he told us this story a number of times throughout his life. Dad said public hangings were outlawed after this.

At the Hall Ranch, the family had a small sawmill, grew their own food, and raised some cattle. Grandpa Hall also had a very famous root cellar that he had dug into the mountainside. Dad often spoke of Grandpa's accident on their ranch. The story is that one day, when Dad and Uncle Hugh were still living at home, a pile of lumber fell on Grandpa Hall and broke his back. His two young sons moved him, and in doing so, did more damage. Dad explained they did not know anything about first aid at that time. Grandpa's back never did heal properly, which made him a bit cranky, especially around a noisy kid like me.

Grandma Hall made up for everything, though. I loved her dearly and had a fondness for her home-canned green beans. Whenever we went to visit, she always made sure to serve them for dinner. One thing I didn't care, for though, was that every time I had a cold, she would try to dose me with Vicks VapoRub. I would run away and hide in the coat closet until she gave up!

Grandma and Grandpa Hall lived on the ranch until August 25, 1925, when a forest fire burning near Beaver Lake (also known as Upper Little Slocan Lake) quickly turned into a crown fire after being fanned by high winds. The fire spread northeast up the Little Slocan Valley, consuming everything in its path. The ranch house, lumber mill, barn, and corrals all burned, except for the animals that Grandpa had let out of the corrals to give them a chance to outrun the fire. According to cousins Innes and Harry, all was lost, including a thousand dollars' worth of hay. Innes said that Grandpa Hall kept running back to the burning house, trying to save some belongings before they finally had to leave with the wagon. Luckily rain finally doused the fire that night, or it would have eventually burned all the way to the Clough Ranch and into Slocan City

After the fire, Grandpa and Grandma decided they would sell the ranch instead of rebuilding. All of their children were now grown with families of their own and the ranch was too much for them to look after between the two of them. Winter would set in soon and they needed a place to live. Mabel, who lived in Slocan City, helped them with a place to stay initially, but she had a small house with a young family, and a winter cooped up altogether would be too much for Grandpa and his bad back. They bought a small plot of land in West Slocan, across the bridge from Slocan City, and built a small cottage. Now that Grandpa and Grandma no longer had the mill or the hayfields from which to make a living, Grandpa needed to find work. He found a cooking job with the CPR on the dredge at Mirror Lake in the summer of 1926, so they bought a fruit farm in Mirror Lake from a man named J. Graham of Perry Siding, and moved to the farm that August. Perry Siding, just south of Slocan City, was about three hours from Mirror Lake in those days depending on the route you took to get there. The settlement of Mirror Lake is located on Kootenay Lake, about twenty-six miles east of Slocan, as the crow flies, though in the mountains, you have to follow the circuitous path of the mountain passes. At that time, to reach Mirror Lake, you took a steamboat, a train, and another steamboat. The shortest travel route would have been to take the steamboat from Slocan City to Rosebery, then a train from Rosebery to Kaslo, then the ss *Moyie* to Mirror Lake and the wagon to the new farm. Mom, Dad, Ray, and I visited them there in August 1927 before making our way up to Cody via first the ss *Moyie* to Kaslo, then the Kaslo and Slocan Railway to Sandon. They farmed in Mirror Lake, and Grandpa cooked on the dredge for about five years. Grandpa also served on the school board of trustees for three years while they lived there.

The dredge was a large boat that consisted of the crew's sleeping quarters, a kitchen and dining area, and the dredger equipment that was used to excavate the shallow lake bottom in and around the wharf so that the ss *Moyie* and other steamboats could pass without scraping their hull on bottom of the lake. It was part of the CPR's maintenance division, so Uncle Wat may have had a hand in helping to find the job for Grandpa.

I was a toddler of about three or four at the time, but I remember very clearly going with my dad to take Grandpa to the dredge in a rowboat. When I saw the water and that we were getting into the little boat I started to scream. Dad picked me up and I wrapped both of my arms around his neck as tight as I could. I screamed my head off the whole way, while he rowed out to the dredge, and the whole way back until I was safely ashore. I did not like going out into deep water. I was terrified that the water was somehow going to get me!

Around May of 1931, Grandma and Grandpa Hall purchased property in the Fairview district of Nelson, where Dad and Uncle Hugh built their parents a home. However, when Grandma and Grandpa Hall left Mirror Lake in 1932 they did not move to Nelson right away. I am not sure whether or not they still had their home in West Slocan but I believe they moved back to the Slocan area for a couple of years while they worked on building the house and to be close by their sick daughter, Mabel. They may have even been staying with Aunt Mabel in Slocan City at that time, nursing her until she passed away. It was 1934 when Grandma and Grandpa finally moved permanently to Nelson, bringing my cousin Ruth with them. Grandpa Hall worked one more year as a cook in Nelson then finally retired in 1936 and joined the Nelson and District Old Timers Association, formed in 1931. At seventy-two, he was already well known by the members of the association.

I remember an adventure I had once while visiting Grandma Hall while they were in Nelson building the house. We were staying in our white tent again while Dad was helping them I was five years old at the time, and Ray was nine. One Sunday morning, Mom sent Ray and me

The author, aged five, in Grandma and Grandpa Hall's backyard, while the house is under construction. Our white tent is in the background at right. Fairview District, Nelson, 1932.

Thomas Brenton and Carrie Hall house on the corner of Sixth and Davies Streets, Fairview District, Nelson, ca. 1934. This house still stands at this same location today. It was the first house built in the Fairview area.

Hall house and garden, September 1938. *L–R*: Lee Hall, Aunt Bertha (née Anderson) Hall, Jennie (née Johnson) Hall, Ray Hall. *Seated*: Grandma Carrie (née Carr) Hall, Grandpa T.B. Hall, cousin Ruth Purney, cousins Beth and Hughie Hall, the author.

down to Nelson Avenue to catch the streetcar to go uptown to the Christian Science Sunday school, on the second block of Baker Street. But when we got to Nelson Avenue, there was no streetcar because it was Sunday. A family we knew (some neighbours of Grandma and Grandpa Hall) came along and offered us a ride uptown. Ray refused the offer and wanted to take me back home, but I said no, that I would go with them uptown. These neighbours happened to be Lutherans, so they took me with them to the Lutheran Church, in a lovely building on the west end of Silica Street that still stands today. (The Christian Science Church building, built in 1928, still stands at 237 Baker Street.)

Ray went back up the hill to tell Mom. I was comfortably seated in the Lutheran Sunday school when the door opened, and who was it but my mom! She had walked all the way from Six and Davies Streets to come get me and take me home! I was somewhat disappointed, but I learned never to accept a ride with either friends *or* strangers.

As I mentioned earlier, the Halls were really the only grandparents that Ray and I knew. Mom's parents, Phylander and Maggie Eliza (Dillon) Johnson, lived far away in Manitoba, and she never went back to visit until I was twelve years old, when she and I travelled to see her mother, who was terminally ill. My Grandma Johnson had not seen me in the flesh since that day she kissed my little pink cheeks goodbye at the train station in Saskatchewan when I was one month old, when she and Grandpa Johnson had come to visit us before we moved to BC. I was excited that I was finally going to get to meet her.

I think grandparents are very important to a child's life—and not just to act as babysitters or provide pocket money! Their stories give you an appreciation for the advancements in industry and technology, and their love always reminds you that you have a place to call home. (My experience told me they always do seem to have more money to spare than parents do, especially pocket money. And you don't even have to ask for it—they just give it to you!).

Dad held the belief that our family's lifespan was about seventy-six years; both his parents passed on about that age. Grandpa died in a Vancouver Hospital in 1940, and Grandma Hall died a year later in her sleep, while visiting Uncle Hugh in Washington. Dad himself lived until he was eighty-nine, which seemed to disprove his idea about lifespans being due to heredity and to prove that one should never limit one's thinking. This difference in lifespans over one generation constantly surprised him.

Mom was ninety-two when she passed away. She would not appreciate my disclosing this information, because she never considered herself to be aging. Maybe that was because Dad was her junior by a few years. I once asked him why he did not marry a younger woman. He thought every man should marry a woman older than himself—that way, even as he gets older, he will still be stronger and able to look after his wife instead of her having to look after him. That was his unselfish philosophy, and it worked out that way for them. They were married over sixty years. Their remains are in the Nelson Memorial Park Cemetery, at the crest of a hill looking westward to the Kootenay River and mountains.

MY MOM, JENNIE Irena Johnson, the prairie girl turned mountain girl, was of pure Irish descent. She never minded the move west; she, too, was used to hardy, pioneer living conditions, and she liked the mountains.

Mom's grandfather on her mother's side, John Dillon, was born around 1820 in Ireland. As a boy, he was sent to America by his mother, as an endeavour to save his life after his brother and father were both killed in a religious conflict. He married an Irish lady named Sarah, who had also immigrated to America. They had three daughters: Maggie Eliza, Sarah Letitia, and Rebecca.

We were not close to the Dillons in Ireland. In fact, our Canadian family was not very popular with the Ireland branch of the family, to say the least. The Dillon family had a hundred-year lease on a castle in Kilkenny County, Ireland. Around 1893, the time came for the lease to be renewed, and a male heir of John Dillon's was required to make claim to the castle. At the time, the oldest male was Mom's brother, Herbert (Bert) Phylander Dillon Johnson. Bert had not yet turned twelve years old, so he could not make the voyage alone to Ireland, and as there was no money to send an adult with the boy, there was no one who could lay claim to the castle. The upshot was that the family back in Ireland lost the hundred-year lease on their home and had to leave. It was not a happy time for either family.

It seems that both sets of Mom's grandparents, the John Dillon family and the Ira Johnson family, came to Orillia, Simcoe County, Ontario, within a few years of each other between 1864 and 1870. Mom's ancestors on her father's side, the Johnsons, came to America on the early ships, settling on land close to the Canadian border in the northern part of Pennsylvania. The family lived there for generations leading up to the American Revolution. They joined the United Empire Loyalists after

Maggie Eliza Dillon and Phylander Johnson's wedding
photo, Orillia, 1882. G.E. WHITEN, PHOTOGRAPHER

American rebels came into their home and set their house on fire with hot coals from the fireplace. The rebels burned their home and belongings, even grabbing items from the family's hands as they were trying to escape and throwing the items into the fire. The Johnsons had to flee for their lives that winter with near to nothing. Ira Johnson's great-uncle ran for almost two miles in the snow with his bare feet to warn neighbours to grab what belongings they could and to hide because the rebels were coming, pillaging and burning everything they came upon. In 1772, the family headed north, crossing the Iroquois River (the St. Lawrence) and settled first in Quebec for about two generations before Ira Johnson's father, Richard, moved the family to Perth Road, Ontario. My aunt Ada claimed they were direct descendants of the United Empire Loyalists.

Johnson family photo: *L–R*: Phylander, Jennie, Grace,
Bert, Marjorie, Eliza, and Edna, in Orillia, ca. 1899.

In the summer of 1870, Ira Johnson and his brother-in-law Owen
Clough purchased a tract of Crown land in northern Orillia, Ontario. They
cleared enough land for a house and cabin, then built a small cabin with
the timber before Ira returned to Perth Road in the fall to sell the old
farm. Ira sent the rest of the family ahead by steamboat from Kingston to
Toronto, where they took a passenger train as far as Orillia. Owen picked
them up from the train station and drove them the rest of the way by ox
cart to the new homestead. The family all lived in the small cabin while
the house was being built. Ira and his eldest son, Phylander, my mom's
dad, drove a horse team and wagon with all their possessions and supplies
for the new home from Perth Road. Phylander was fourteen years old at
the time.

As the farm grew, they planted an apple orchard and built a cider mill,
selling the fruit, cider, and vinegar throughout Orillia and the adjacent
county. They also sold cream, grain for milling flour, maple syrup, and
wood cut from the land. Here another son and two daughters were born
to Ira and his wife, Mary Grace Clough, who had immigrated to Canada
from England at age six. There were eleven children in all: Phylander,

Almena Jane, Alfred Owen, Alice Melvina, Sidney Herbert, Samuel Frederick, Lyman Harrison, Albert, Edwin Charles, Ella Augusta, and Ada Irena Cora. Phylander married Maggie Eliza, the eldest daughter of John Dillon, on January 30, 1882. Sidney married Sarah, the second-eldest daughter, several years later.

In 1902, Phylander moved his family west to Manitoba, first to Glenora then in 1904 to their new homestead four miles south of Greenway, where he and Eliza would live until their death. In 1905, Ira died on the farm in Orillia, in the house he and his family had built. Mary Grace died in 1912, while being cared for in their oldest daughter's home. Ira's son Edwin took over the farm first and then sold it to his brother Frederick in 1909. Frederick and his wife lived there until their deaths in 1936, at which time son Elmer inherited the farm. The Johnson family farmed the North Orillia homestead for over one hundred years, spanning three generations, before Elmer finally sold it in the 1970s.

I think I acquired the flair for adventure from listening to the stories about my pioneering parents and my other ancestors. Mom told me one story about her youth during a warm summer evening in Greenway. She and another girl were wandering about with a couple of young fellows when they spied a "speeder." (A speeder is a small, flat railcar driven with a hand pump, also known as a hand car or a pump trolley.)

Well, the boys decided to "borrow it" to take the girls for an evening ride. As they were merrily pumping the trolley down the tracks and Mom and her friend were enjoying the ride, the pumper, who was facing toward the direction from which they came, was startled to see a light appearing in the far distance on the tracks, travelling in their direction. The boys began to pump the speeder faster and faster, but the light kept coming, getting larger and larger, close and closer. By now, Mom and her friend were getting a little hysterical about a train chasing them and having no way to get off the speeder because it was rolling too fast. Then they realized it was all just an illusion, the train was really the full moon rising directly in line with the railroad tracks. I bet they all felt pretty silly and had a good laugh after this good scare.

I learned three things from Mom's story. One, that when it came to me playing on railroad tracks, I came by it honestly. Two, some things you just have to laugh off and not get embarrassed about. Three, sometimes things are not what they seem to be and it's all just in your own mind.

Author at one and a half years old, Sandon, 1928.

4

EARLY MEMORIES

WORK MUST HAVE been scarce for Dad in Sandon at times. Although we had moved there in November 1927, Dad would still need to take short-term jobs elsewhere, which took us away from Sandon, sometimes for a couple of weeks or months at a time between 1930 and 1931.

A few early memories stand out for me from when I was between about two and four years old, with a head full of curls. Once, we were living in a large white tent, with a little woodstove, at Mom's relatives on the Clough Ranch. There were two large houses on the property. Great-Aunt Ada and Uncle Wat lived in one house, and on a hill above lived their daughter Phyllis and her husband, Tracy Cooper, with their young family. Our tent was at the top of this long, big hill between the two houses. I remember running up and down that hill till I was exhausted. For a two-year-old, this was such great fun!

We also lived in this same white tent sometime later, at Appledale, where Dad was cooking at the government relief camp for the men who were building the bridge across the Slocan River. This was just one of several types of camps that Dad would work at over the following years in between mining camp jobs.

The mornings were crisp at the relief camp. I remember that Dad would light a fire in the huge camp cookhouse stove, and while I stood on the open oven door, he would dress me in my day clothes. These are short, fond memories.

Another time, Dad cooked for a relief camp crew that was building the road between Rosebery and Nakusp. This was in 1930. A rough wagon trail led from the north head of Slocan Lake to Nakusp, but the most popular way to travel to Nakusp and Rosebery was by sternwheeler or by the Nakusp and Slocan Railway. Although the railway extended farther south past Rosebery to New Denver, the boats and barges on Slocan Lake met the railroad at Rosebery, not New Denver, probably because Rosebery had a sheltered bay. Rosebery also had a boat slip, where the barges were built and repaired, as was the icebreaker that worked the Slocan Lake during the winter.

Rosebery was also the point where the train moved onto the railway from the barges. There was no rail line between Slocan City and Rosebery, so the train and its boxcars would be loaded onto train barges at Slocan City, ferried up the lake to Rosebery, then unloaded back onto the rails for their journey to Nakusp. At Nakusp, the same thing would happen in reverse: the train would be ferried up Upper Arrow Lake to the CPR junction at Arrowhead and be put back onto the rails to join the CPR.

At that time, the mountainous terrain in many places made building a road or a railway too hazardous, difficult, or costly, so wherever tracks could not be built on the side of a mountain or in a valley, someone would throw in a boat. At Rosebery and Nakusp, the barges and steamboats completed the connection between three railroads, the Columbia and Kootenay Railway from Nelson, the Nakusp and Slocan Railway from Sandon, and the Canadian Pacific Railway from Revelstoke.

While Dad was cooking for the road crew, Mom, Ray, and I stayed at Rosebery with him. Rosebery only had a few houses at that time. Aunt Ada and Uncle Wat had a house there, too, for Uncle Wat's work with the CPR. Phyllis stayed at the house that summer while Tracy was looking after the leg of telegraph line from Rosebery to the head of Slocan Lake, which was frequently damaged by the crews blasting rock above the railway to clear a path for the road. We rented another little house nearby.

We would watch the steamers *Slocan* and *Rosebery* and the tugboats *Sandon* and *Hunter* move the barges carrying goods to Nakusp and the area. When things were quiet and no one was around, Ray and I would play, Ray supposedly keeping an eye on me as I ran back and forth on the station platform where they unloaded the railcars. Once, as I ran by a steel wheelbarrow sitting on the platform, I tripped and fell against a torn edge of the wheelbarrow, hitting the corner of my eye. Fortunately, I don't remember anything more of the incident . . . although I still have the scar to prove it happened.

The road built along Slocan Lake before it was rerouted to
Highway 6. The Slocan–Silverton tunnel to New Denver, ca. 1930.

The steamer *Rosebery* on Slocan Lake, 1925. The Rosebery train station is in the
background, with the Nakusp and Slocan Railway passenger train pulling into the station.
PHOTO DONATED BY PHYLLIS COOPER TO THE SLOCAN VALLEY HISTORICAL SOCIETY ARCHIVES

One other personal memory around this time was also scary. Our family had just seated ourselves in the front end of a fair-sized open launch. As other passengers came on board, we heard the terrified yelps of the launch owner's large dog, which had its bushy tail caught in the flywheel of the engine. Sadly, I can't recall how things turned out for this dear creature, or the fate of his bushy tail.

After spending the summer in Rosebery, we travelled to Slocan City and took room and board at the Madden House, across from Aunt Mabel's. Dad continued to cook for the road camp. The work crew must have started in the spring at Hills on the north end of the Slocan Valley

The steamer *Slocan* on Slocan Lake approaching the wharf at New Denver, ca. 1900.
She is pushing a train barge on her way up to Rosebery from Slocan City. The peaks
of the Valhallas are hidden in the fall cloud cover. BC ARCHIVES, C-06314

and worked south toward Slocan Lake, because Dad was working in Hills
and logging at Box Lake before we were in Rosebery. Ray was seven at
this time and started attending school in Slocan City with our cousins
that fall. I was three, so I stayed home with Mom. I remember watching
Mom wash laundry while I chewed wheat berries that I had stolen from
the chickens. I would chew the berries until they became soft and turned
into this great chewing gum, and then I would swallow it. Mom had a big
copper boiler on the woodstove to heat the water for the wash, and a scrub
board out back of the house. She would wet the clothes thoroughly and
rub the bar of soap on them, then scrub the wet soapy clothes on the scrub

The steamer *Slocan* at the wharf at Rosebery. The train barge had been docked and the railcars are ready to be unloaded and rejoined to the train, 1913. BC ARCHIVES, A-00674

board. Then she would rinse and wring out the clothes and hang them on the line outside to dry in the fresh air.

During my younger years, New Denver was the hub of the area. From there, you could travel in all directions—north to Nakusp, south to Slocan City and Nelson, east to Sandon, where the population in the once booming mining town was now outnumbered by New Denver, and west across the Slocan Lake to the gorgeous views of the Valhalla mountains and glaciers. I really loved the high mountains, with their glaciers shining in the sun.

New Denver always seemed to be a place that took us somewhere else, as we never seemed to stop there very long—just long enough to shop a bit

The CPR junction at Arrowhead on Upper Arrow Lake where the railway cars and engine would be transferred back on to the railway after being ferried up the lake, 1896. *Foreground:* A barge with ore from one of the mines is being ferried in to transport the ore to the smelter. *Background L-R:* A barge docked off the wharf with ore from Halle Mines is being unloaded in to the railcar to be transported to the smelter; Arrowhead rail station; CPR passenger train from Revelstoke. BC ARCHIVES, H-00595

while waiting for a train, or a steamboat, or a ride to the Clough Ranch. Our friends from Sandon, the Tattrie family, were from New Denver. It was also the home for many Japanese Canadians who were interned there during the Second World War, and to a number of Japanese Canadians who chose to make it their permanent home after the hostilities were over. Although New Denver's claim to fame seems to be as an internment camp during the war, I remember it as the lovely town that pointed you in all directions, sending you on to new places and new adventures.

Photo taken in 1919 by Lee Hall from the Noble Five looking down toward Cody, a small silver mining settlement at the base of the tramline tower. Cody was surrounded by hundreds of mining claims.

5

SANDON

D AD TALKED A lot about the Noble Five mine. It had been closed for a number of years and was now reopening. I think Dad must have taken a job cooking for the mine, because we moved to Cody in August 1927, when I was six months old. The mine was located above Cody, a small settlement centred around the confluence of Carpenter and Cody Creeks, just a short distance up the mountain from the town of Sandon. The Noble Five had a concentrator and flume in Cody and aerial tramlines that ran down from the mine above.

We did not stay at Cody for very long. By November, the heavy winter snow had already set in, and Dad and Mom decided to move us down to Sandon to a house up on a hillside called Sunnyside Bench. Later, Dad and Mom bought a building that had been Dr. Gomm's office and moved us down lower into town. Sunnyside had been warmer than down by Carpenter Creek, but the creek area was safer in the winter because it was a little farther from the snowslides that were always a major concern.

Dr. William Edward Gomm, born in 1866 in Savannah, Georgia, immigrated to Canada from California in 1895. He settled in Sandon around late 1896, opening a private physician's practice on Reco Avenue and boarded at Black's Hotel. In summer of 1900, just after marrying his second wife, Maude Beadleston, in a ceremony at Nelson, he purchased the Lane cottage on Cody Avenue next to Carpenter Creek and moved his private practice into the attached office. There he raised a family and held several different public office positions over the years on Sandon's city council. In 1910, he was also the elected mayor of Sandon. He was Sandon's local physician and surgeon and the primary physician for the

Houses on Sunnyside, top row, in Sandon, 1929. In 1920, Mom and Dad's first
house had been the fourth house from the left. In 1927, our house was the third
from the left. Not much had changed in the seven years they had been gone.

Dad in front of our old house (Dr. Gomm's office) in Sandon, ca. 1975.

Miners' Union Hospital, the hospital built in 1904 up on the mountainside above our house on Reco Trail. It was the fourth hospital building of the Union, as the prior three were destroyed or their structure considered unsuitable for a hospital. The Miners' Union Hospital group was established December 5, 1898, by the miners, and the first hospital opened in August 1899. Dr. Gomm was generous with his services to the miners for twenty years before he gave up his practice in Sandon and took a coroner position in New Denver in 1920. He sold his house to the Boates family. Dr. Gomm was a prospector at heart, investing in and developing two successful mines in the area, the Get-There-Eli and the Ya-Ya. Dad knew Dr. Gomm from the years when he had been working in Alamo and driving ore wagons down to Sandon for Mr. Cunningham.

The house we lived in was originally attached to the back side of Dr. Gomm's residence, in what had been his office for his private practice. Years after the Boates family purchased his house, they decided to separate the office from the residence and moved it across the road to its present-day location. I believe this happened in 1928, when Dad purchased the building. Moving the building was quite a feat. It was separated from the main house then raised up with timber blocks so that it could be eased down onto a skid. Then it was pulled in a wide arc by a team of horses to rotate it into place across Cody Avenue from Dr. Gomm's old house. The little office then became our new home.

Sandon is located about nine miles up the valley from New Denver at the confluence of Carpenter and Sandon Creeks. It is very close to Alamo, where Mom and Dad were married. The mountains in which Sandon is nestled are filled with ore. Most of the mines in this area yielded mostly lead-zinc ore and a lead-silver ore known as galena. The silver was the real money maker.

Young as we were, the names of the mines were well known to Ray and me. In Sandon, we grew up with names like Surprise, Freddie Lee, Sovereign, Reco, Slocan Star (Silver Smith), Eureka, and Ruth Hope, as well as terms like single jacks (four-pound hammers). Then there were the Viola Mac Mine, the Rambler Caribou, and the Famous Payne Mine, the original silver strike of 1891 that started it all and gave rise to Sandon.

We did not live in Sandon in its heyday. Dad had worked at the concentrator at Alamo Siding and hauled some ore when he was courting Mom, but he never did work underground, because he was a camp cook. I'm glad, as I know too many men who ended up with silicosis or were killed in mining accidents. Working underground and driving a team of horses down the mountain with a heavy load were dangerous jobs.

For the first two years we lived in Sandon, Dad mostly worked for Mr. Cunningham as a cook, and then again in 1932 as a compressor manager at one of his mines. During the three years in between, Dad took over the proprietorship of the Exchange Café on Reco Avenue. Dad loved to cook, but I do not think he enjoyed running a business, because he never purchased another business again. The Exchange Hotel and the Exchange Café were two of the oldest businesses in Sandon and had changed ownership many times in their first thirty-five years.

Clarence J. Cunningham was an American mining man from Alaska who arrived in Sandon about 1916. In those years, Mr. Cunningham leased and bonded a number of mines whose ore veins had run out near the surface and had shut down because prospectors did not want to pursue the ore veins deeper underground. Mr. Cunningham's idea was that one mine that produced ore could carry the others until ore was found in another one. Mr. Cunningham's properties were the mill at Ruth; the Sovereign, the Wonderful, and the Miller Creek mines at Sandon; the Queen Bess and Idaho-Alamo mines above Alamo Siding; the Van Roi and Hewitt mines at Silverton; and the Fidelity Group at Trout Lake. Dad worked for Mr. Cunningham for many years at several of these properties.

Dad respected Mr. Cunningham, who he said was a very nice, kind, generous man. He was very good to his employees. Dad recalled in a letter (see appendix) some years later that Mr. Cunningham "used to ride a saddle horse from one mine to the next [on] a rangy Chestnut [named] Rex that would walk the roads and trails at four miles an hour." Later on, Rex fell on Mr. Cunningham and broke his leg. It eventually healed but he didn't walk quite the same afterwards.

Although Mr. Cunningham had made over a million dollars from the mines, the Great Depression was not kind to him. Mineral values had drastically dropped and mining activity in Sandon had almost completely stopped. The concentrator in Alamo was barely keeping busy with the product from his own mines. Mr. Cunningham spent the remainder of his fortune by continuing to invest in his mines to keep them operable, accumulating a large amount of debt in the process. He shut down part of his operations and lived out the rest of his days with his trusted housekeeper and bookkeeper in the beautiful mansion that he had built for himself around 1918 at Alamo Siding. Dad's long-term employer and friend passed

New concentrator at Alamo Siding, 1919, built by Clarence Cunningham in 1918–19.
The Nakusp and Slocan Railway, from New Denver, is on the left. On a bench above and
behind the concentrator, Cunningham had built a lovely mansion surrounded by
English gardens overlooking valley and railway. BC ARCHIVES, D-01977

away in 1938, penniless but well remembered and respected by his friends
and those who worked for him.

Mom loved to write on photos. It didn't matter where she made her
notes, on the fronts or backs; she wrote down names, places, dates, or in
general marked someone with the all-important "X." On one photo of Sandon, taken around 1932, she noted that Dad had been running the kitchen
at the Reco Hotel for Johnny Harris. During the Depression, many mines
had shut down, so this may have been the only place to cook in town. I was
in my first year of school, so Dad would not uproot us until the school year
was over.

JOHNNY HARRIS (REALLY John Morgan Davis from Vernon Mills, Virginia) was another American with big ideas, and arrived in the area
around 1892. He was a man of wealth and many talents. He had founded
and developed Sandon and was the noted owner of the upscale Reco Hotel.
He also owned much of the townsite and utilities, and was a prospector

The Hall house, in 2004. The Petersens' house was next door
on the right. Their house was always painted white.

Ray, almost five years old, in front of the Sandon CPR train station, January 1928.

and owner of the successful Reco mine. He is well noted in Sandon's historical records.

Dad told me more than once that Mr. Harris had told Dad he had shaved Wyatt Earp the morning of the gunfight at the OK Corral in Tombstone, Arizona. I never heard whether Mr. Harris revealed this to anyone else or not, but Dad's word was always trusted by us kids. Whether it was true or not, we loved these types of stories—after all, we had no televisions back then. Our house was next to the old Kaslo-Slocan Railway Station. I remember the house well. It had three small rooms: a kitchen, a living room, and one bedroom, with front and back porches. The exterior of our house, like most of the buildings, was just grey, weathered shingled siding boards. I don't remember our house ever being painted. The road in front of our house was Cody; it followed Carpenter Creek up to the settlement of Cody, at the base of Cody Mountain. We didn't really have a yard, as there wasn't much room in the narrow valley with both the creek and a road and houses on both sides. There was just enough yard room behind the house for the woodpile, a shed, and a backhouse. Hidden behind the shed was a little narrow alleyway to nowhere. This was my secret fairy garden, my own special little world and my most favourite place to dream and play. I called it Huckleberry Lane because it was full of huckleberry bushes, buttercups, and other wildflowers, everything needed to make houses that could attract fairies. I never knew why the lane was there until I was older and saw a partial townsite map of Sandon in Garnet Basque's book *West Kootenay: The Pioneer Years*. The lane had apparently been the siding for the Kaslo and Slocan Railway. When the K&S was leased by the CPR in 1912, they abandoned the K&S station in Sandon and the narrow-gauge railway on Sunnyside. The K&S was then rebuilt as a standard-gauge rail that tied into the existing Nakusp and Slocan Railway, which stopped at the Sandon CPR station on the opposite side of Carpenter Creek, downtown by the business section. I guess I was never aware of this when I was little because the fairies had erased all remnants of the railway from my secret lane once they had taken back their land.

Our neighbours across Cody Road were the Boates family and the Tattries. The Boates family lived directly across from our house, while the Tattries lived up the road three houses. The Towgood family lived next door to us on the lower side, in the old renovated K&S station. They were packhorse freighters and kept a teaming livery stable. All of our neighbours had at least one person who worked in a mine, but the Tattries had a general store downtown too that Ethel Tattrie ran.

When I was small, the road between our house and the Boates's seemed really, really wide. Before Sandon was used as an internment camp, I returned there with Uncle Wat and Dad. It was my first trip back as a teenager, and I could not believe how much the road had shrunk. Dad teased me, saying it was all in my mind and that it was me who had changed in size, not the road. He also told me the road had been built only large enough for an ore wagon and a team of horses to pass through—the houses came later. How our impressions of size change with time!

The small, white, well-kept house next door to ours on the upper side belonged to the Petersens. The Petersens had two girls. One of the daughters and I were about the same age. Mrs. Petersen used to make a Norwegian treat called krumkaker, which resembled an ice cream cone. The krumkaker was a thin cookie cone with a lacy design on it, filled with whipping cream and berries or sometimes a custard pudding with jam. On the days when she made those, she let each of us children have one as a special treat, which was very nice because there were a lot of us! We had lots of playmates, five or more children from the Boates family, and the Tattrie's girl.

Sometimes the Petersen's aunt would come to visit. She was from California, I think. The last time she visited, I had been playing with her niece when she promised she would mail a doll to each of us as soon as she got home. We waited with great anticipation. One day they came: mine was a "Patsy" doll made by the Effanbee Doll Company, and there was a note with it. The note explained that this doll had belonged to her little daughter, who had died some years before, so I have always treasured this gift. I still have it today, these many years later. I had new clothes made for her, copies of the originals, because the others had disintegrated with age. My friend's aunt sent her niece a lovely new doll, which she loved too. I wonder if her doll is as still treasured as mine is today?

Mom, Dad, and Mr. and Mrs. Boates loved to play cards together, bridge being their favourite game. I liked to stand on the back of Mom's chair while they played; that is where I learned the importance of the ace of spades. One evening, while perched over her shoulder, I spotted the ace of spades in Mom's hand. In my excitement, I hollered, "Mom's got the highest card in the deck!" There was a great laugh, except from Mom, and then I was banished into the room where the rest of the kids were playing games. When we got home, I also received a short lesson on what card playing was all about. I think I lost most of my interest in card playing around that time, "'cause that wasn't much fun!" Playing cards can get you into trouble in more ways than one.

On another evening, when I was four, Dad told me to go up the road and fetch a chicken for supper, as the neighbour had one for us. I do not

My 1928 Effanbee Patsy doll, a gift to me from my neighbour's aunt.

recall if it was to the Tattries or the Petersens that I went, but when I got there, the neighbour chopped off the chicken's head and handed me the rest of it. I was walking back to our house, carrying the chicken by the leg, when it jumped out of my hand, stood on its two feet, and ran into the bush. I screamed for Dad. He came running out of the house, asking me what was wrong. I said, "The chicken ran with no head into the bush." It was all so very frightening. Dad consoled me, then went and fetched the chicken from the bush, and Mom made supper.

Sandon had some of the fiercest storms I have witnessed in my entire life. I don't ever remember being afraid of thunder and lightning, even as a small child, but there is one particular storm that still stands out, from when I was about four. It was a hot summer day and we had been visiting the Lane's residence on the other side of our narrow valley. Donald Lane and I were close in age and would often play together while our mothers visited. His father worked at the Ruth Hope mine. I remember

Postcard of Sandon, 1933. The Miners' Union Hospital is the large white building with a flat roof on the upper road (Reco Trail). The boardwalk, named Main Street, ran between the two rows of buildings on the lower roads (between Reco Street, left side, and Slocan Star Street, right side). The swift waters of Carpenter Creek ran beneath the boardwalk. City Hall is the second building from the bottom on the row of buildings to the right.

playing inside the house that day and hearing the booming rolls of thunder. I looked through the window and was overawed at the display of immense jagged streaks of brilliant light over the mountain top above our little home, which was nestled in the valley below. It was amazing to me, it was so grand and beautiful!

While we lived there, Sandon had one flood that I remember, in the year 1929. There were two creeks, the Sandon and the Carpenter, which joined at the top of the boardwalk. This boardwalk, Main Street, was built above the swift waters of Carpenter Creek and began just about a block below our house. As the creeks roared down the mountain valleys with heavy snowmelt, the force of the water brought down large boulders in both creeks at the same time and piled them up at the top end of the boardwalk, tearing out planks and timbers.

All the women and children were sent to the Sandon Miners' Union Hospital while the men fought the flood. The hospital had recently been closed due to the Depression, but all the blankets and linens were still there, plus the wheelchairs, beds, etc. I was about two at the time, and Ray was six. I can still see him and his pals in the wheelchairs racing around the hallways, having great fun. Of course, the rowdiness did not last long, especially with the echoes in the emptiness of the building.

Years later, Bill Boates, my friend from across the road at that time, told me that one day his dad had had a terrible toothache but couldn't get to New Denver for medication. So his dad went up to that old Sandon Hospital, closed for over twenty years by then, and opened up a medicine cabinet. And lo and behold, there was the medication he needed! This really shows the honesty of the people of that period: nothing had been stolen or vandalized in all that time.

One of my little friends was the Tattrie girl, who lived up Cody Road on the creek side. The Tattrie home was built very close to Carpenter Creek—in fact, I remember my friend's mother, Ethel, hanging out her washing from a small porch that jutted out over the creek itself. One day while she was hanging out her wash, the railing broke and she fell into the fast-flowing water and was drowned. It was a sad time for us all. I think my little friend was taken down to New Denver to live after that. Their house later became the Tin Cup Café, which burned down in 2008.

I don't know if it was for Ethel Tattrie's burial or not, but Dad took me to the cemetery on the hillside at Sandon about that time. It was in June of 1933, near the end of the school year. It was my first education on death and burial. I have always connected this with Ethel Tattrie's accident.

My first conscious awareness of my existence and of things around me was when I was in Sandon. I was sitting in my baby buggy, and two girls were pushing me down a narrow lane behind our house. I was sitting up in the carriage, so I must have been about nine or ten months old. Of course, it was just a brief moment, a quick vision, but one I have never forgotten. I must have noticed something magical about that hidden lane even then— perhaps it was a fairy that caught my attention. The summers in Sandon are more in my memory than the winters, even though the summers were much shorter; it was probably because the children had more freedom to be outside in summer.

Sandon was considered home for my first six years, even when we followed Dad to other camps for his cooking jobs from time to time. My memories of Sandon include my first year of school, which was located on the top floor of the city hall. I started in the fall of 1932. It was the year the government decided children had to be six years old before starting school; I was only five that September, but someone in authority felt that because my birthday was in February, I should begin school anyway. I was ready! Ray had already been going to school for four years. All the classes up to grade eight were held in the same room at the same time and taught by one teacher.

Our schoolteacher was a man; it may have been his first school assignment. I say that because my first memory of that day was one of astonishment. One of the little boys was being noisy and misbehaving, and the teacher walked over to him, picked him out of his seat, one hand under his chin, the other on the back of his head, and shook him like a rag doll. Needless to say, I was scared to pieces it might happen to me. My first year in school was spent learning how to count up to one hundred. I found out all you had to do was to change the first number in the table and you could count forever and never run out of numbers; you just let one number follow the other. It gave me a great feeling of accomplishment!

I do have one other memory about school from that time. One day, I was returning to classes after lunch and as I was entering the building, I looked down and saw that I still had on my pinafore (apron), which I had put on to eat my lunch. I was so embarrassed, I began to cry and ran back home for some mother-comfort. That was my only school year in Sandon, because the next year we had moved to Beaton, where I entered grade two.

In Sandon, the common method of mining was to find a surface vein of ore, then blast the rock holding the ore. The broken rock would then be sorted into one pile of ore and one pile of the waste rock, which had to be moved out of the way. The ore would be sent to the mill for processing, and the waste rock would be dumped down the mountain slope to what was called the "mine dump." The miners repeated this process over and over, following the ore vein deeper and deeper into the mountain, creating tunnels up to hundreds and thousands of feet deep. Inside the

My first schoolroom, in Sandon, was on the top floor
of the city hall, built in 1900. Photo taken in 2004.

tunnels, the ore cars on rail tracks moved the blasted rock outside to the sorting table and waste rock to the dump. Some of the mines, typically the big operations, used power to move the ore cars to the exterior, but if you were a small prospector you usually moved your own wheelbarrow or maybe had a mule pull the ore car for you. Mules that worked in the tunnels were known as mine mules or pit ponies.

Bill Boates, one of my playmates from Sandon, once told me an amusing little story about a mule that worked in one of Sandon's mines. The miner who owned this mule would have it pull the heavily laden ore cars out of the dark mine tunnel to the exterior. There was no electricity in the tunnel to light the way, so the miner used a carbide lamp on his hard hat to light the tunnel path before him. Even the miner's mule had his own carbide lamp. Because it was dark in the tunnel and the mule could not see where he was going without his lamp lit, the mule would refuse to go into the tunnel until that was done. Smart, stubborn mule! Bill said that after the mule was retired from mine work, he would go to the school each day to meet all of the kids as they came out of the building when school was done for the day. Bill said the mule could always be heard braying a little before the end-of-day dismissal. Who ever said that mules are dumb?

We left Sandon summer 1933; by that time, the mines had closed and there were only about fifty residents left. I think Mom and Dad had intended that we would return to Sandon again, because we did not sell our house. Years later, when we were living in Nelson, Dad wanted to know what had happened to our house in Sandon. To my knowledge, the Canadian government just walked in and took over Sandon during the Second World War and never notified us about our house at all. As I mentioned earlier, in 1942, after the bombing of Pearl Harbor, the War Measures Act gave the government authority to move all people of Japanese descent inland, away from the Pacific coast. As a kid, I did not understand the politics of this: I was simply told that some Japanese people living in Canada whose loyalty to Japan was in question started the whole thing. Sandon, although mostly abandoned from the Depression, still had a running power plant, water, heat, and many usable structures to house people in, some of them even furnished. Sandon also had a school, a hospital, a ball park, and a skating rink. However, it was also isolated because the terrain was very mountainous and had only one road into and out of it: an ideal place for the government to send internees. Over nine hundred Japanese-Canadian men, woman, and children were relocated to Sandon. I cannot begin to imagine how they felt, but it must have felt even worst to live in such a remote place against one's will. The mountains to me had always represented unlimited freedom, beauty, and adventure. How utterly different could our two experiences be!

When Dad went to check on our house, he found a Japanese-Canadian family living in it, a woman with her elderly father and two children. He spoke a little with them and then left, but before he was too far down the road the woman came running after him and pushed a small purse of money into his hand. Dad was a very compassionate man and would have given them the house, but the family insisted that they buy it from him. During his service in the First World War, Dad had seen plenty of good people caught in a bad situation through no fault of their own. The family gave him all the money they had, one hundred fifty-cent pieces. Dad sold them the deed to the house for fifty dollars. I am not sure why he accepted the offer; perhaps he recognized the woman's need to gain back some dignity and control over her life, and perhaps it made her and her family feel a little more like normal free citizens to own their home. Whatever the reasons were, that family and others following must have taken good care of it, because the house is one of the original homes still standing today, withstanding over one hundred years of Sandon snow. It is still privately owned.

Today, Sandon is a famous ghost town and a popular tourist destination, especially with historians. A few people still call it home, and there are still some old buildings standing, including Dr. Gomm's office, Petersen's house, the city hall, and the Silversmith Powerhouse, which still generates power today. It is the oldest continually operating plant in Canada. The Tattrie home has since burned down, as has the Boates home. The Sandon Historical Society runs a museum out of an old brick mercantile building that was once the general store under the proprietorship of Tattrie and Greer while we lived there.

The Stainton boys getting ready to ride in a parade to commemorate the Silver Jubilee of King George V, Trail, BC, 1935. Freddie Stainton (my future husband) is on the left. Older brother Lionel is on the right, little brother Keith is in the middle. Note the pictures of King George V and Queen Mary on Lionel's bike handle bars. The Staintons lived next door to the United Church in Trail.

6

BEATON

WHEN WE LEFT Sandon in 1933, I was six. Mom and Dad had some money saved by then and had to decide whether to buy a car with their money and temporarily go on government relief until Dad found another job or to live off their savings. They chose the former, so we now owned a 1931 or 1932 four-door Pontiac sedan.

Mom, Ray, and I went back to the Clough Ranch while Dad rustled up a new job at some other mine he had heard was opening up. Word was, a Vancouver company was reopening the Meridian Mine, above Camborne, and building a mill with a water-power system. The Lade brothers, Jim and Vince, the mine's previous managers, would be the manager and foreman again. Dad was contracted to cook for the Meridian camp, but the job would not start for another month or so.

It was during this time, before we moved to Beaton, that Dad took a short-term job on a sternwheeler that had been sold to a gentleman and was being used as a tourist attraction. The ss *Kuskanook* was moored at Kokanee Landing on the West Arm of Kootenay Lake, where her staterooms were used by vacationers. Dad was cooking for the guests.

On one particular day, I guess I gave everyone a pretty good scare. Ray had been playing with a boy his age who was also staying nearby the landing that summer. The two of them decided they were going to take a rowboat across the bay to a beach called Sand Spit, just around the corner of the bay from Kokanee Landing. The boys wanted to go and find the Boy Scout camp at Kokanee Creek that they had heard about. I said I wanted to go too, but Ray was always trying to dump me, as one tries to

The author, six years old, and brother Ray, ten, in 1933.

do with little sisters, and told me that I had to stay behind. I replied that I was going to tell Mom, and then neither of us would get to go, so he took me. They rowed over to Sand Spit, a sandbar that you can walk out on for about a quarter of a mile. We played there all afternoon. When we finally headed back to the ship, it was around suppertime. As we came around the bend, I could see a woman in a bathing suit diving off the main deck of the ship. It wasn't until we reached the ship that we found out that she was looking for me. We had not told anyone where we were going, and when they couldn't find me on the ship, they thought I had fallen overboard. We all caught heck.

Before school started that fall, we were on our way up to the end of Upper Arrow Lake to a little town named Beaton. I never questioned our moving around; I just went with my brother and my parents wherever "that" was. I have always been very grateful they never left me behind. I know of children who were left behind to be raised by relatives or others while their parents went on adventures or to work in other locations—not my mom and dad! Dad would always find us a place to live with him or

Boy Scout troop at Camp Busk, Kokanee Creek, West Arm of Kootenay Lake, ca.1934.

one close by and collect us from the ranch after he had our belongings sent to his new job location. This latest move was an adventure, as we travelled by boat and train to Nakusp and then sailed on the paddlewheeler the *Minto* past the towns of St. Leon and Halcyon Hot Springs to Arrowhead. There we met Captain Soules, who ferried us up the arm to Beaton on his tugboat *Beaton*. I really don't remember the ride, probably because I hid my head, trying not to look at the water. (I didn't learn how to really swim until I was twenty-six, and then only in a swimming pool.)

Arrowhead was the junction where the CPR trains from Revelstoke met the supply and passenger boats on the Upper Arrow Lake. Captain Soules had a tug and a barge, with which he picked up passengers and goods at Arrowhead to take to the settlements at the head of the Beaton Arm.

I don't know who paid for the expenses every time Dad moved us to a new place, but I suspect it was whatever mine hired him. I do know he had an expense account for the miners' food, and that he asked for decent, substantial food to cook with for the miners. That was why he was a popular cook. Dad believed the men needed good food, and they appreciated him for it.

The steamship *Kuskanook*, on the West Arm of Kootenay Lake, part of the CPR.
A.D. Pochin purchased the *Kuskanook* in 1932, hoping to turn the boat into a floating hotel.
In 1933, it was moored at Kokanee Landing and used as a tourist attraction. Eventually,
the waterlogged wooden hull gave out, and it sank in 1936. The remains of her
wooden hull can still be seen today at low water. BC ARCHIVES C-06309

Upper Arrow Lake, ca. 1944. The paddlewheel steamer *Minto* and the tugboat *Beaton* are docked. The *Beaton* and its barge were owned and operated by Captain Soules. The CPR's passenger car is on the left, pulled up to the *Minto*. Photograph by E. Dickey, Revelstoke. BC ARCHIVES B-00043

The town of Beaton was located on the Beaton Arm of Upper Arrow Lake; it was the doorway to the mining town of Camborne, six miles up a deep, winding canyon wagon road that followed the Incomappleux River. The Incomappleux River (Fish River) is a swift and turbulent waterway, which courses down the canyon and empties into the Beaton Arm of the Upper Arrow Lake.

When we arrived in Beaton, Dad already had a house set up for Mom, Ray, and me, since he had to go on to the Meridian Mine above Camborne to start work right away. We stayed in Beaton so that Ray and I could attend school, because there was no school in Camborne. I guess Dad got some days off, because he came down to Beaton once in a while. I remember Mom and I would wait with him on the front porch for the wagon to take him back to Camborne. Once he got there he would still have to climb the narrow steep trail that was the only route to the mine.

Meridian Mine, above Camborne and the Incomappleux River, 1933.

Children of the Kootenays

We rented a nice two-storey house with a porch. The house was close to the school and community hall. The snow would be very deep in the winter, and we kids would climb out of the bedroom window and slide down the porch roof to land in the snowbank below, then take our snow-laden bodies back through the house to try it again, until Mom said, "That's enough!"

It was time to go to school again, so I started grade two; I guess Ray was in grade five. With all the moving around we did, sometimes it was difficult to tell what grade Ray was in; wherever we were, though, if there was a school nearby, Mom would make sure we attended it as long as we were in the area. Early on, before I was of school age and Dad was cooking for the relief camps in Slocan, Ray would sometimes go to school with our Clough cousins. When I was older, and if we were visiting them during the school part of the year, I would go to school with them then too.

In Beaton, Miss Jean Balderston was our schoolteacher from 1933 to 1934. The school was close to our house. I remember walking to school in winter on cold crisp mornings and hearing wolves howling, so I was glad it was just a hop, skip, and jump to get there. Actually, I loved to listen to the wolves howling and singing. One would start and then another, and another. Sometimes it sounded like they were all around you. I do not remember hearing the wolves howling like that in Sandon, nor in Camborne, nor anywhere else during my lifetime.

Like all small communities, the school had a Christmas concert to entertain parents and friends. Of course, everyone came, including the babies. This took place in the community hall, which was next to our home. I remember playing the part of "Little Miss Muffet who sat on a tuffet" and got scared by a spider. Brother Ray played the part of a sailor in another skit at the concert.

We children had a grand time, but a sad memory of that night was of two young men, the Cashton brothers from Winnipeg, who were coming to Beaton for the Christmas party. They had been working at the Teddy Glacier Mine, which was across the river and northwest from Camborne on Mount McKinnon. They were travelling on the road with two pack horses when a snowslide came down in front of them and blocked their path. When they turned to go back, another slide filled the road that way too, and then the third slide caught the men and horses, forcing them down the mountain to their deaths. The search party found them a few days later. Doubly sad was that we heard one of the young men was engaged to a young lady in Beaton.

I gleaned this information as a six-year-old not only from the conversation around me but also by my asking Dad, who always answered all my questions. And I truly was always asking Dad questions, even trivial ones, such as, "Why do you always cut your sandwiches from corner to corner or crossways, instead of in halves like Mom?" Dad's answer was, "So you have a point to stick in your mouth." "Oh!" was my reply, for it did not make sense to me at all. Dad once asked me why I asked so many questions. I replied, "How am I supposed to learn anything if I don't ask questions?" My questioning never bothered him again after that.

It was the end of summer 1934, and we were still living in Beaton when the news came that Mom's father had passed away in Manitoba. This was my Grandpa Phylander Johnson, whom I had never really known. The only picture I have of the two of us is of Grandpa holding me in his arms at the train station in Greenway, Manitoba, when I was two months old, before Dad and Mom moved our family out west. For Mom to go to the funeral, she would have to take the tugboat to Arrowhead, a train to Revelstoke, and then another train to Winnipeg, where someone would pick her up in a wagon and take her to Greenway. For whatever reason, Mom did not go to the funeral; however, she and I did visit Greenway five years later, just before my Grandmother Eliza Johnson passed away, in 1939.

THIS PERIOD OF Beaton's history was described in *Silent Shores and Sunken Ships* by Milton Parent, which was published in 1997. I sure am glad he wrote it, because it restored my faith in my own memory about things no one else seemed to write about.

In Beaton, the Evans family had a farm and a number of children. The boys delivered milk to Beaton and Camborne. I once was at a sleepover at the Evans place, with the two Evans girls of my age, Marion and Winnie. It was a night to remember. We three all had to sleep in the same bed. I had never slept in a bed with two other people before. The biggest decision was who was going to sleep in the middle. Why, the guest, of course! Well, I had never been so warm in the mountains in all my six years.

The Evans boys had a big German shepherd. One winter day, I was on the road near our house and I saw the boys and the dog coming toward

Beaton's one-room log school in winter as seen from shovelled pathway, early to
mid-twentieth century. ARROW LAKES HISTORICAL SOCIETY ARCHIVES, 000-035-1

Mount McKinnon, ca. 1935. The Teddy Glacier Mine was true to its name: it was on a glacier!

me. I had heard that the dog was rather mean, and as I had been making a snowball, I thought I had better get rid of it, or the dog might think I was going to throw it at him. I guess he did think it, because he came at me full speed with the boys running after him. The dog went for my hand, but, thankfully, I had my mittens on, so I was not really hurt—though I'm sure my screams reached every ear in the town. It goes without saying, I have been cautious of this breed of dog ever since. We never had a dog of our own when I was growing up, probably due to our many moves. It is possible the German shepherd just wanted me to throw him a snowball and play, and I just panicked.

Doris Harlow, a young woman from Nakusp, came to look after Ray and me so Mom could go up to the mine with Dad once in a while. Mom needed to go to Nelson for a whole month once, so Doris took Ray and me to her parents' farm in Brouse, near Nakusp. Because of the length of time we stayed there, we attended the Brouse School. One day in class, we were asked to write a descriptive paragraph. I learned a lesson I have never forgotten to this very day, which was to not use so many "ands" in my writing; I have thought of it incessantly while writing these stories.

Doris had a brother for Ray to follow around. One of the older boy's jobs was to set out traps to catch coyotes. One evening, the whole family went for a walk and decided to check the traps. One of them had a young coyote in it. To this day I can still see the look in that animal's eyes; it knew exactly what was going to happen, and it was so very afraid. Doris's brother shot it, and I was devastated—it was so awful. Despite that incident, we did enjoy our stay at the Harlow farm. Doris took good care of us, and the Harlows were a nice family.

One other incident comes to my mind from when we were at the Harlow's place. I had always loved mashed potatoes for dinner—so much, that I would take a slice of bread, cover it with the potatoes, and fold it over into a sandwich to eat. Everyone laughed at me, but I did not mind. It was good, and it was my own invention.

When we got back to Beaton, we were getting ready for another move. I don't know if maybe there had been nowhere else for us to live in the rundown mining town of Camborne before, or if travelling back and forth between Beaton and Camborne was getting too tiresome for Dad, but we moved there that summer, even though there was no school for us to attend in Camborne. I'm sure our parents gave that some thought, but Mom fixed it by finding a teacher from Revelstoke who would come and home-school us.

Coal-oil lamp from my childhood;
it gave us light and warmed our home.

7

CAMBORNE

CAMBORNE WAS A gold-mining settlement located at the confluence of the Incompappleux River and Pool Creek. It was August of 1934 when we moved the six miles up to Camborne from Beaton. We had some furniture, so Dad must have borrowed a horse and wagon through the mining company to move our belongings. We had very little furniture that moved around with us, just the essentials: a bed for Mom and Dad, one for me, and the Winnipeg couch. The Winnipeg was a folding metal-framed couch that converted to a bed at night and back into seating for the daytime. Ray slept on this for many years, until we moved to Sheep Creek, when he finally got his own bedroom. The rest of our furniture consisted of a dinner table, four chairs, a cast-iron cookstove, our Roger's cabinet radio, and two coal-oil lamps. The coal-oil lamps were our only light in the evening. Both lamps sat on the table and were lit at dark and, along with the cookstove, helped keep the room warm during the long winter evenings. We travelled light, with only a few personal items, linens, and clothing, Mom's sewing machine, and the necessary cooking utensils and dishes. The large kettles that we always kept filled and readily heated on the back of the stove were some of our most important possessions.

We mostly burned wood for our source of heat, or coal, when it was available. Coal lasted so much longer, but you had to buy it. The forests around us provided plenty of wood from fallen trees, so there was no shortage of it to burn in the cookstove or heater, plus wood was free. Getting the wood into the house was Ray's job; mine was to carry in the kindling.

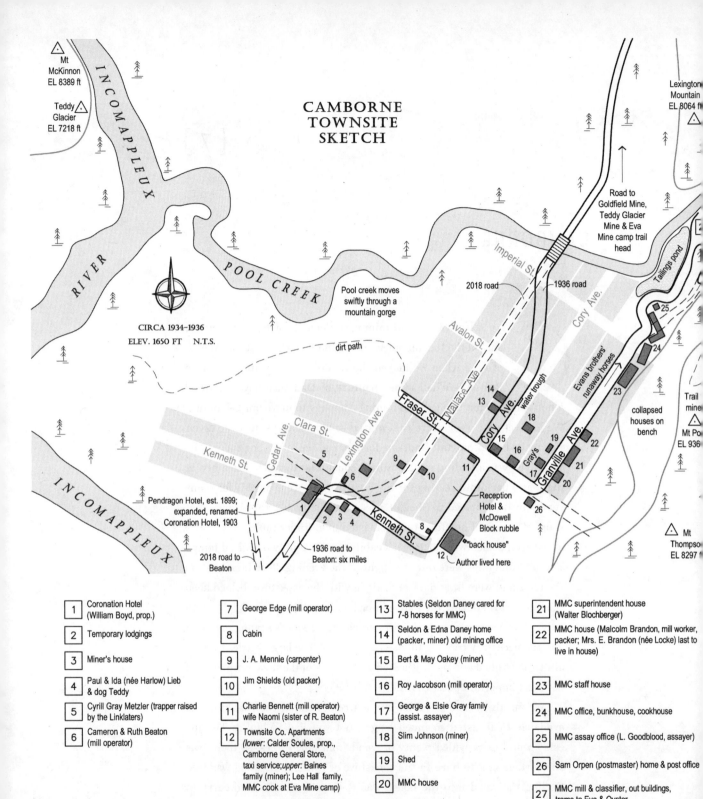

CAMBORNE TOWNSITE SKETCH

Mt McKinnon EL 8389 ft

Teddy Glacier EL 7218 ft

INCOMAPPLEUX

RIVER

POOL CREEK

Pool creek moves swiftly through a mountain gorge

CIRCA 1934–1936
ELEV. 1650 FT   N.T.S.

dirt path

INCOMAPPLEUX

Lexington Mountain EL 8064 ft

Road to Goldfield Mine, Teddy Glacier Mine & Eva Mine camp trail head

Tailings pond

Imperial St.

2018 road

1936 road

Cory Ave.

Avalon St.

water trough

Evans brothers' runaway horses

collapsed houses on bench

Trail mine

Mt Po EL 936

Fraser St.

Wallace Ave.

Cory Ave.

Granville Ave.

Clara St.

Cedar Ave.

Lexington Ave.

Kenneth St.

Grays

Reception Hotel & McDowell Block rubble

Mt Thompson EL 8297

Pendragon Hotel, est. 1899; expanded, renamed Coronation Hotel, 1903

1936 road to Beaton: six miles

2018 road to Beaton

Kenneth St.

"back house"

Author lived here

MMC superintendent house

Mt

Sketch of Camborne Townsite, ca. 1936.

1 Coronation Hotel (William Boyd, prop.)

2 Temporary lodgings

3 Miner's house

4 Paul & Ida (née Harlow) Lieb & dog Teddy

5 Cyrill Gray Metzler (trapper raised by the Linklaters)

6 Cameron & Ruth Beaton (mill operator)

7 George Edge (mill operator)

8 Cabin

9 J. A. Mennie (carpenter)

10 Jim Shields (old packer)

11 Charlie Bennett (mill operator) wife Naomi (sister of R. Beaton)

12 Townsite Co. Apartments (*lower*: Calder Soules, prop., Camborne General Store, taxi service;*upper*: Baines family (miner); Lee Hall family, MMC cook at Eva Mine camp)

13 Stables (Seldon Daney cared for 7-8 horses for MMC)

14 Seldon & Edna Daney home (packer, miner) old mining office

15 Bert & May Oakey (miner)

16 Roy Jacobson (mill operator)

17 George & Elsie Gray family (assist. assayer)

18 Slim Johnson (miner)

19 Shed

20 MMC house

21 MMC superintendent house (Walter Blochberger)

22 MMC house (Malcolm Brandon, mill worker, packer; Mrs. E. Brandon (née Locke) last to live in house)

23 MMC staff house

24 MMC office, bunkhouse, cookhouse

25 MMC assay office (L. Goodblood, assayer)

26 Sam Orpen (postmaster) home & post office

27 MMC mill & classifier, out buildings, trams to Eva & Oyster

The Coronation Hotel, Camborne, 1935, one of the few larger
structures still standing in 1936. The Townsite Apartment Building
was a long building and looked very similar to the three-storey
portion (right) of the Coronation Hotel for its full length.
ARROW LAKES HISTORICAL SOCIETY ARCHIVES, G-17-04-06

These were the days when you were rich if you could afford a battery
for your radio. I can still see that radio in my mind's eye and hear the
laughter broadcasting from the *Fibber McGee and Molly* comedy show.
We also had a black cabinet gramophone. It had a handle that you would
wind up to make the record disk go around, so no electricity was needed.
It was there that I would watch Mom's rapture as she stood listening to the
Victrola after she received her first hearing aid. If it sounds like we were a
little poor, we never felt it.

As with all mining towns, nothing was ever permanent. By 1934,
the buildings in Camborne lay mostly in ruins. Mom, Ray, and I lived on
the second floor of the three-storey old Townsite Apartments, the only
apartment structure in Camborne, built around 1903. When it was built,
it was unique to Camborne because it had small living suites complete
with cookstoves, instead of just a single sleeping room like in a hotel or
a boarding house. Our apartment had only two rooms—a place to cook
and eat with a little sitting area and a bedroom. There was no bathroom.
When we had to go we used a chamber pot, which we emptied out later,
or we trekked downstairs to use the outhouse. In the winter, trips to the
outhouse were carefully planned because the seat was so cold. We used

Town of Camborne seen from Meridian Mine, 1934. We had to hike the
narrow switchback trail to go to see Dad at the cookhouse for Christmas.

another room in the building for our school classroom. The building was warm enough in the winter, after all—the walls were insulated with sawdust and empty whiskey bottles!

During the winter evenings, Dad usually stayed up the mountain at the Meridian Mine cookhouse, and Ray and I would play cards or with games or toys, while Mom read. One evening, in the dead of winter, I was having an argument with Mom that I could not win, so I declared I was going to run away. I was expecting words of protest from my mom and brother, but instead Mom calmly replied, "All right, I'll pack you a lunch." That really ticked me off—after all, I was only seven! I looked outside, where it was snowing big BC snowflakes and the snow was deeper than I was tall. The trip outside no longer appealed to me: it looked cold and wet, and it was pitch-dark. No street lights, of course. "Well, to heck with it," I thought; no one seemed to love me enough to want to stop me from going, so I would punish them both. I'd stay home!

Meridian Mine crew, at tunnel entrance to Eva or Oyster claim, Camborne, 1933. Archie Oakey, top left; Paul Lieb fourth from top right; Ragnar Olson second from top right; Paddy Morin third from bottom right. Note the mule for pulling ore carts inside the mine; it has its own miner's light on its chest. ARROW LAKES HISTORICAL SOCIETY ARCHIVES, 2017-012-1-12-3

DAD WAS A wise man. He told us that if we ever got lost in the mountains, we should always listen and look for a creek or stream and follow it downhill. Why? Because people always live where the waters gather, and that is where you want to be to get help. If you didn't, you could end up a long way from home. Fortunately, I never needed to use that knowledge.

Mom sometimes used to take Ray and me up to the cookhouse at the Meridian Mine for the day. The hike was about a mile of switchbacks up the mountainside. We loved going up to see Dad. All the mines we lived near had similar living conditions. Because of the number of men who were single, there would be a bunkhouse and, of course, a cookhouse with a large dining room. Usually there would be a separate bedroom for the cook in the cookhouse. The "flunky" and the "bull cook" probably bunked in the bunkhouse with the rest of the miners. The bull cook was not really a cook. He was the fellow who did the heavy chores for the cook, such as seeing that all the garbage was put out or burned and bringing in the supply loads when they arrived by the freighter's packhorse supply train.

I can't remember how many miners had to be fed—maybe fifty. When Dad had their meals ready, the flunky, or second cook, would call the

Meridian miners' camp above Camborne, ca. 1935. A travelling photographer took many panoramic pictures around the area and sold the developed photos to the miners. *Buildings L–R:* The bunkhouse, wash house or cook's quarters, outhouse, cookhouse, shed. The entrance to the Oyster Mine claim of the Meridian is located on the hillside above the centre power pole. Standing by the cookhouse dressed in white is Selby Soules Jr., flunky, and Lee Hall, camp cook. WALTER RING.

miners to their meals, using the metal triangle with a rod hanging from it outside the cookhouse door. The flunky would take the metal rod and hit the inside of the metal triangle in a circle, making a great clanging noise that could be heard all over the area. The bunkhouse doors would open, and the men would head for the dining hall. Dad and his helpers would eat their meals after the miners had finished theirs. Mom, Ray, and I would join Dad if we were visiting at mealtime.

Selby Soules Jr., one of Captain Soules's sons, was one of Dad's helpers in the cookhouse, working as a flunky. Selby was also the flunky when Mattie Günterman was camp cook at the Meridian, before Dad took her place. Ray and I liked Selby, who was a young man. Some of the miners became good friends to our family, especially Paul Lieb's family, who were also with us in Sheep Creek in later years. Like many of the other Scandinavian miners, they often seemed lonely for their families back in Norway and Sweden and took a liking to Ray and me.

It was fun being at the cookhouse kitchen. All the mixing bowls Dad used to make cakes were enormous, and Ray and I couldn't wait to clean out the leftover cake batter from a mixing bowl, as Dad was generous with what he left in the bowl for us. Mom always scraped the cake-batter bowls out more when she cooked at home.

Closeup of Selby Soules Jr. and Dad at Meridian Mine in winter 1935.

I never had a hearty appetite. One explanation for this was that I used to sneak chewing gum before dinner. Dad always kept packages of spearmint chewing gum in his club bag. He was a slim man and preferred to remain so, and the gum curbed his appetite. Dad did not want to look like the usual heavy cooks or chefs; he claimed that their extra weight came from tasting all their recipes. Anyway, I loved chewing this gum too, but every time I did, it spoiled my appetite and I would not eat my dinner. Mom would ask, "Shirley, have you been into Dad's gum again?" Silence was always my best bet. I learned at a very young age to tell the truth, because the only time I told a lie, Dad caught me at it. I decided right there and then that I would never become a liar, as I could not remember what I had said, but I could always remember the truth.

When we were at the cookhouse, we tried to help Dad with small jobs. I remember twelve-year-old Ray trying to carry a box of heavy dishes and dropping the whole box. I don't think he broke many dishes though, because they were thick and heavy, but Ray sure felt upset about it.

One thing I noticed about the other cooks at different mines was that they always wore a head covering in their kitchen (restaurant cooks did too), but Dad never did: he had no hair that could fall into the soup. Cigarette ashes wouldn't fall in there either. Our Dad seldom, if ever, drank alcohol or smoked tobacco. Only twice did I ever see him accept a smoke from anyone, and then he never finished it. I am sure if I asked why he did not smoke, he would have said it did not go with the food in the kitchen. Once he told me about restaurants he had gone to where he could see into

Meridian miners' camp, above Camborne, Christmas 1934. *On roof of cookhouse:*
miners; *back row in front of cookhouse, L–R:* three miners, Paul Lieb, Bert Oakey.
Back row in front of shed, L–R: Demers dressed in white (flunky), miner, Carl Carlson.
Front row, L–R: Archie Oakey, Jock Denny, three miners, Oscar Noackson, Gordon Green,
eight miners, Ernie Larson, miner, C. Erikson, miner, Jack Fraser, Tom Boyter, Selby Soules,
Geo Baines, Scotty Gray, Lee Hall dressed in white (cook), Ragner Olson, Carl Olson.

the kitchen, and there would be the cook stirring a large pot with a cigarette in his mouth and a two-inch ash hanging off it ready to fall into the pot. I know what he meant; I have seen it too. This was why he refused to eat in certain restaurants.

On Christmas Day in 1935, we climbed the hill to the mine through the snow, to be with Dad for Christmas dinner. We must have gone up later in the day, because I do remember opening our presents from Santa

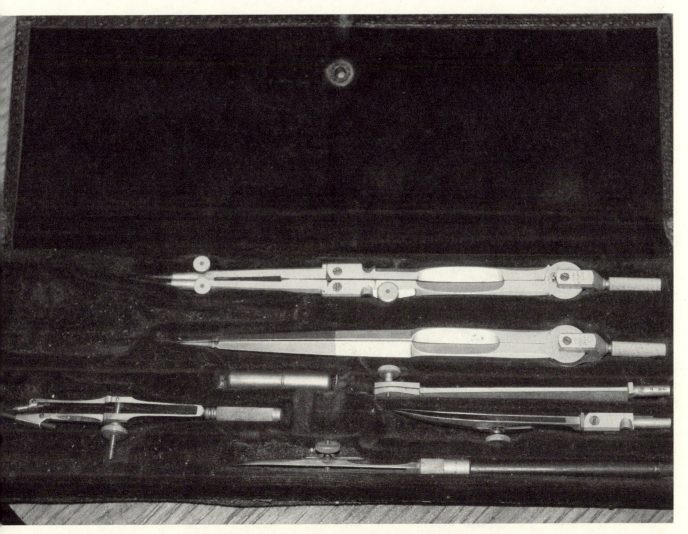

Compass set, a Christmas gift from a miner to Ray in 1935. The miners were generous to us, even though they did not have much and had no family close by.

Claus at our apartment in Camborne that morning. Ray had asked for a toy caterpillar, and I had requested a toy racetrack with greyhound dogs racing each other around in a circle at the turn of a handle. Of course, these choices came out of the Eaton's catalogue, but my friend Betty Baines and I were determined to believe that Santa had brought them.

Up at the mine, the miners gave us kids Christmas presents too. Some men left the mine for the holiday, but the majority stayed at the bunkhouse, since their families lived in other countries. One of the men whose family still lived in Scandinavia gave Ray an expensive compass set. I am sure it was the miner's own. This set sits in a drawer of my desk these many years later. The gifts we received from the other men were coins, but

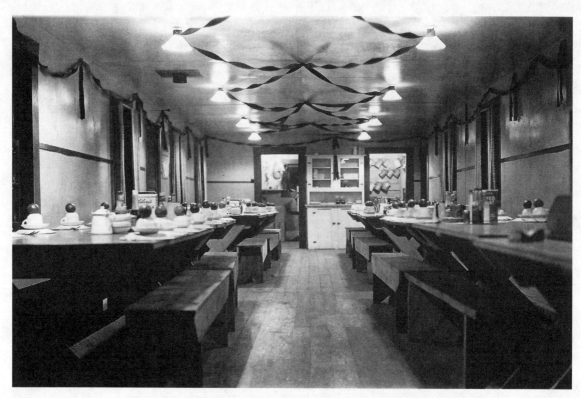

Inside the cookhouse, this was an example of Dad's Christmas morning tradition for the miners. This table was set for Christmas breakfast at the Kootenay Belle Mine in Sheep Creek, 1936. It was a novelty for us to see an orange.

I don't know what they would have bought us, since there was nothing to buy for kids in Camborne anyway. I don't know if any of the men actually did ever get back to their home countries again, but I do know a few of them travelled on with us to the next mine that opened.

At Christmas, Dad always set up a special dining room for the men. The breakfast table was always set the previous night. First, the big plate went face down on the oilcloth table cover, then the saucer face up on top, with the cup upside down on the saucer, and lastly, a big orange on top of it all. Ray and I thought it was just great! It was a novelty for us to see an orange, especially at a mine site. No matter how rustic and small, or how grand the dining hall was, this was Dad's Christmas tradition at all the mine cookhouses.

Soon after Christmas, Calder Soules, Selby's brother, opened up a little store on the bottom floor of our apartment building. He named it the Camborne General Store. At first there was not much in it, but as more people

Road to Camborne from Beaton up the Incomappleux
River Canyon, 1935. BC ARCHIVES, NA-11328

Camborne miners' kids: the Grays (George, Grace, and Gifford)
with Jean Boyter in front in the white dress, 1935.

Jimmy Brandon with pack horse, freighting lumber to the Meridian Mine to build
a new bunkhouse at the Eva claim. The wood had to be cut to shorter lengths to make
it transportable by horse. The Meridian Mine comprised six mining group claims
above Camborne. The Eva and the Oyster were the main working claims, located
on the southwest slope of Lexington Mountain. Dad cooked for both at the
Eva miners' camp. ARROW LAKES HISTORICAL SOCIETY ARCHIVES, 2014-003-1793

requested goods the little store grew in size and merchandise. I remember
that he had to take down some of the interior apartment partition walls
on the bottom floor to make a large enough space for the counters and
shelves. Inside, he had a little office/apartment to the right and a storage
room at the back of the store. He also bought a car that he used as a taxi
between the towns of Beaton and Camborne. It has taken me some time
to unravel our transportation system between Beaton and Camborne, as
I don't remember ever getting a ride in a vehicle. I don't remember us having our car at Beaton, or at Camborne, so we must have left it at Slocan
with relatives. There had been no one to help me solve the transportation
question until I found Florence Baines, a younger sister of my friend Betty
Baines, who lived there with her family at the same time as we did. Flo and
her little brother, Billy, were born in Camborne. Flo said we travelled on
foot or by horse and wagon in the summer and on foot or by sleigh in the
winter. Camborne was only about six miles from Beaton (just over nine

and a half kilometres). People walked a lot in those days, and what seemed to me a long way to walk as a child was not that far to walk for an adult. Walking was a necessity then, not exercise.

The first time I remember seeing or drinking pop was at Calder's store. It was called "Gassosa." My little friend Jean Boyter called it Gassola. Gassosa was manufactured in Trail, BC, at the Gassosa Pop Company, which started production in 1923. The pop was in a strange glass bottle with a bulge at the top that held a marble to seal the bottle. I presumed the glass ball was pushed up by all the gas bubbles inside and sealed in the liquid pop; however, it was a mystery to us children. To be able to drink the pop, we had to get the marble loose to break the seal. We did this by pushing the marble in with a finger or hitting the top of the marble with a stick, then the marble would sink inside the bottle. We called this "popping the marble" because the bottle would make a popping sound when the gas pressure was released. I later found out that this strange glass bottle is called a Codd bottle. Sometimes the boys would not return the bottles to Calder's store. Instead, they would break the bottles to get the marbles out for playing shooting games with them.

The schoolteacher Mom arranged to home-school Ray and me, because there was no school in Camborne, was Claire Balderston, a young woman from Revelstoke. She moved into our apartment building. I believe she was the younger sister of Miss Jean Balderston, our schoolteacher in Beaton. We enjoyed being home-schooled very much. Miss Claire took us for nature walks every morning before class. I loved those morning walks, with all the stillness of the forest, the wildflowers, and the little animals, as well as the big ones. I remember the walks well; especially the time we found a snake that had just swallowed a mouse!

One day during class, we saw a bear cub wandering around the building by itself, which usually meant that a mother bear was nearby; when you live in bear country, you are taught that fact when you are very young. In spite of that, Ray, who was eleven, decided to chase the little fellow, who, of course, immediately climbed a nearby tree. Miss Claire, our mom, and some others came out on the back porch to see what the ruckus was about. They were all calling Ray to come in because mama bear was sure to be out there somewhere, but Ray was fearless. Fortunately, mama bear knew her cub was safe, and our cub listened to *his* mama and came back into the building.

Workers attempting to clear path through a snowslide blocking road along the Incomappleux River four miles above Beaton toward Camborne, winter of 1934-35 (Caterpillar licence reads 1934). The snowslide was thirty feet deep (a tree was notched, and the depth was measured in the spring). *L-R*: Paddy Morin, Lee Westland, Seldon Daney, Ollie Berg. ARROW LAKES HISTORICAL SOCIETY ARCHIVES, 2014-003-1653

Ray used to love to "help" the Brandon brothers load the pack horses for the trips up to the mine where Dad was—though I am sure he just watched! Once, a bear frightened the horses on the trail and one of the horses fell over the side of the mountain. That was when I learned that horses were very scared of bears. The Brandon brothers were from Beaton and had a freight and packhorse train outfit. They would contract with mining companies, prospectors, and townspeople to haul in equipment, food, and building supplies into areas that were difficult to reach by boat or train. They usually travelled the high single-track trails for horses and wagons through the mountains, routes that were steep and often slick and muddy. It could be a very dangerous job. Malcom, the oldest brother, married Jean Balderston, my schoolteacher from Beaton, in 1940.

I think my memories are clearer during my Camborne years because I was learning so many new things. I even began to disbelieve in Santa Claus, though Betty and I still pretended to believe for each other's sake (even though she was four years older than me). Betty Baines and I lived

Gracie and Gifford Gray,
Camborne, 1935.

next door to one another on the second floor of the apartments, so naturally we were playmates; actually, I don't remember any other girls our age being there. Betty's family really loved Christmas. Her little sister, Flo, told me that their mom wanted a Christmas tree so badly that year that she took down their bed and put up a tree in its place.

One Christmas holiday morning, Betty and I were sitting outside in the fresh snow, discussing Santa Claus and whether he was real or if we were being fooled by our parents about his existence. I guess this was all part of learning to distinguish between the real and the unreal. We came to the conclusion that we were not ready to give up believing in Santa. We decided we would believe in him for one more year. As I mentioned earlier, Santa used the Eaton's catalogue to give us our gifts. We would pore over its pages sometime in November for ideas of what we would like for Christmas. I do not remember getting an extra present from Mom and Dad—Santa was it—so you can understand why Betty and I had to work out this question carefully; the following Christmas would have to look after itself.

That particular Christmas, I got the toy racetrack with the aforementioned metal greyhounds racing around on it. I could turn a little handle

Meridian Mine, upper terminal of the tramline, winter 1935. Below the tram to the right is the town of Camborne at the confluence of Pool Creek and the Incomappleux River. The waste from the Meridian Mine was dumped over the edge of the mountain, in plain view above the town. In the distance is the Beaton Arm of Upper Arrow Lake.

on the side, and the little dogs would race each other. We must have cared for our toys in those days, because when I was fifteen, that toy was still in the attic of our house in Sheep Creek. When my family moved from there, my toy was left behind. I hope someone else found it in the attic and enjoyed it as much as I did. Brother Ray's present from Santa that year was a caterpillar, just like Seldon Daney's.

Seldon Daney! He was a beautiful, handsome man with gorgeous blond hair. And with a name like Daney, I assumed he was a Dane. Anyway, I adored him from afar, since I was about eight years old and very shy. When he teased me, I would hide behind my dad's wide pant legs, which shielded me from anyone's sight, but I liked the attention. Seldon used to drive a big "cat," or some other large piece of equipment. In the wintertime, the snow on the road would get very deep. The tractor had no blade, so Seldon would run the tractor's big metal tracks over top of the snow, packing it to make the road passable.

Seldon was married to Edna (she was Mrs. Daney to us). We were taught to always address an adult using Mr. and Mrs. or Miss. This was considered proper etiquette if you were a kid and speaking to or of someone not in your immediate family.

The Daneys were one of the young couples who were going to have a baby, and around that time, the Jock Denny family just had a new baby. Babies were another topic Betty and I had to do a lot of thinking about— from where, when, and how did they arrive? Other young couples in Camborne already had babies, so we girls had the pleasure of having little babies around to enjoy.

The Evans family had a dairy farm across the Incomappleux River from Beaton. Their boys delivered milk up to Camborne. Mom had been giving us children condensed, tinned Pacific-brand milk diluted with water to drink. It was not unpleasant tasting, but I was having some kind of problem with sores on my legs, which the doctor said was caused from not drinking fresh milk. The reason we were using the tinned milk was because there was no electricity in the apartment, hence no refrigeration except for an icebox. The tinned milk was pasteurized, so it did not need to be refrigerated like fresh milk, but the pasteurization process also destroyed a lot of the vitamins and minerals fresh milk had. This is why companies producing condensed milk started to fortify, or add vitamins, back into their milk. Mom changed over to fresh milk, and that was the end of the problem.

After a delivery of fresh milk, every couple of days, we usually drank it so fast that it didn't have a chance to spoil, and if it did go sour Mom would bake with it. Other items we needed to keep from spoiling we kept in our small icebox, which was our refrigerator. It was a wooden cupboard with a couple of shelves that had a special cupboard at the top for a place to store a block of ice, and the cool air from the ice would sink down to the lower compartment. Ice blocks would be made in the winter or cut from freezing ponds and stored in sawdust in a cellar or ice house for use in the summer. We would purchase the ice from someone when we needed it.

In the winter, the Evans boys would drive their sleigh up to Camborne, pulled by two rather high-spirited horses. I remember them as beautiful blacks, and I loved to look at them. One day, the boys stopped at Scottie Gray's house, where Mom and us kids were visiting. Mom and Elsie Gray were friends in Camborne. The Evans boys went inside, leaving the horses unattended. We kids were all playing outside when Ray and the Gray boys talked me into climbing onto the back of the sleigh. I was game, but scared. I had planned on just sitting quietly, but the boys started making clicking noises to the horses. The noise made the horses take off at a dead run, with me hanging on for dear life, crying and screaming at the top of my lungs. I was all of eight years old. Ahead of the bolting horses was the Meridian Flotation Mill, at the base of the tramline that came down from the mine; this was the end of the road, after which a roaring creek came tumbling down the mountainside. Despite the noise of all the machinery in the mill, the workmen heard the commotion and ran out to the road, where they were able to stop the racing team just in time from going into the creek. I jumped to the ground and never stopped running. I have no idea how far it was back to where I started. I don't even remember what the punishment was that the boys suffered, but there were lots of scared people— most of all, me! To this day, whenever I see a movie showing a team of horses out of control, I know just how the passengers feel.

MY PARENTS WERE what the world would call "ordinary" people. I would call them a good example of upstanding souls: law abiding, always doing their best, intelligent, and completely trusted by others. We always trusted our parents to do their best for us, and we knew they loved us. But believe me, if we stepped out of line in doing or speaking wrongly, a sharp cuff across the ear from Dad (which, thankfully, happened seldom) was swift and sure. Dad told me he had spanked me every day for the first two years of my life. I never remembered getting even a single spanking, so I wonder if that is even true. However, I remember when I was screaming away in my high chair, Dad simply picked up chair and child and put us both in the closet and shut the door. I immediately stopped my crying. The closet door was soon opened and I was out, probably without another tear.

Small children learn early in life that parents fret a lot. It could be because they often worry you are dead when you are not. At least, that is my opinion.

WORKING IN THE mine was dangerous. Once, a man was seriously hurt in the mine and a doctor was sent for. The closest one was far away, in Revelstoke. This meant the doctor had to travel by train from Revelstoke, take the tugboat from Arrowhead, then a wagon ride from Beaton, and then the doctor was sent up on the tramline in an ore bucket to the mine. The last part of the trip would be the scariest, maybe even worse than a runaway team of horses. I did not like the way the buckets rocked. Sometimes, I used to look up at those buckets swinging high in the air and wonder what it must have felt like to ride in one. I don't remember hearing if that injured man recovered.

Although there was always the possibility of injury for the workers in the mines, no one thought there was danger for the camp cook. One day, Dad was cutting meat for supper in the meat safe. (The meat safe was a small-screened shed outside the cookhouse where Dad stored the fresh meat. I think there were ice blocks stored in sawdust that kept the meat cool, since there was no refrigeration up at the mine.) While carrying out an armload of meat, his knife slipped and cut his hand badly; Dad had huge butcher knives that he always kept very sharp. The wound required some urgent first aid and possible surgery. Dad had to get down the mountain, take a wagon or walk to Beaton, then a tugboat to Arrowhead, where he would have to take the train to Revelstoke, or wherever he could find medical attention. This was in the summer of 1935, so the hospital was no longer functioning in Arrowhead. Ray, Mom, and I remained in Camborne anxiously awaiting his return.

I don't recall much more about that incident, except that when Dad came home with a big bandage on his finger, he had presents in his club bag for each of us kids and for Mom. My present was a mug with pictures of England's King George V and Queen Mary, so this accident must have happened around the event of King George's Silver Jubilee. I still have the mug among my treasures, so I suppose I was allowed to use it only on special occasions. I remember that the king of England's picture always hung on our school wall and in the post office.

GRANDMA AND GRANDPA Hall were living in Nelson by that time. We went to visit them periodically. Our trips entailed taking the tugboat from Beaton to Arrowhead to catch the sternwheeler *Minto*, and then travelling down the Upper Arrow Lake to Nakusp. The *Minto* was much like her sister ship, the *Moyie*, which is now a Canadian national historical site

My special gift from Dad: a mug commemorating the Silver
Jubilee in 1935 of King George V and Queen Mary.

in Kaslo. Although I did not like travelling on the water very much, the
Minto was big and pleasant, so I could run around on it all I liked.

After arriving in Nakusp, we would take the train to New Denver,
where one of our relatives from Slocan City would pick us up and take us
to the Clough Ranch for a visit. Often it was Uncle Wat or Mom's cousin,
Phyllis Cooper, who would come for us. Our car was stored at the ranch,
so we would then drive to our grandparents' home in the Fairview district
of Nelson. I think there was a bus service between Nakusp and Nelson at
that time as well, but I don't remember ever taking it. It would take us
most of the day to travel approximately 140 miles (225 kilometres) from
Camborne to Nelson.

Mom had bought a little, pale-blue velvet sailor hat for me—which
I loved! On one trip to Nelson, I was wearing my beautiful hat. As usual,
I wanted to go out on the deck to watch the *Minto*'s approach into the dock
at Nakusp. I asked if I could go alone, and Mom said I could. Of course,
the wind had to be blowing, and as I watched the wake from the paddle-
wheels, the wind lifted my precious sailor hat from my head up and over
the paddlewheel falls. My last sight of the hat was of it floating on the
top of the foam from the paddlewheel, sailing back the way we had just
come. I ran back inside sobbing to Mom, but I could not be comforted. She
promised to get me another one and later purchased something similar,

The *Minto*, winter, ca. 1898. It was from this steamship in 1936 that I watched my precious blue velvet sailor hat float away on top of the foam from the paddlewheel, back the way we had just come. BC ARCHIVES, A-00658

but it was not my blue velvet hat; maybe she could not find another one just like it. I think I am permanently scarred from that experience, as I have never forgotten that little blue velvet sailor hat.

IN CAMBORNE, WE had a very poor mail delivery system; it sometimes took many weeks for letters to arrive. This upset Mom, as she was so far from her family, so she wrote a letter to the post office asking why the mail took so long. Their only excuse was that there was something like six other towns in British Columbia called Camborne. Sounds fishy to me. It was a good thing Santa knew where we lived!

One of the best things that ever came in the post was a parcel from our Aunt Grace, Mom's sister, who lived in Saskatchewan, where Ray and I were born. Despite the looming Depression, Aunt Grace had kept their farm near Spooner, when Mom and Dad decided to sell theirs. Aunt Grace would send us crates of eggs, home-canned chicken, and other goodies. The egg crates were shipped by train to Nelson first, then to Slocan City.

Cousin Ruth and me, with my new little sailor hat, Sheep Creek, 1936.

The whole train would then be ferried up to Rosebery, put back on the tracks to Nakusp, and then the eggs would travel by boat the rest of the way to Beaton. The eggs were packed in water grass to keep them from breaking. Aunt Grace did this for us for many years, especially during the war years of 1939 to 1943, despite the terrible hardships her family endured on the Prairies.

In all the mining towns we lived in, I don't ever remember having any kind of a garden. I think, for one thing, that the ground was too rocky. Then all the water had to be hauled up from a creek or lake to water anything. Also, the growing time in summers was very short due to the high altitude of the mines. So the mining companies would horse-pack into the mines all the food and supplies needed for the men—although I think the men would fish and hunt some for fresh meat as well. In Camborne, we lived in an apartment, so we did not have a plot of land to grow anything. I am sure these are all just excuses; I don't remember us having a garden in Sandon, either. Maybe some of the people in the outlying cabins, such as the Evanses and the Güntermans, had gardens that I didn't know about.

Mom and the other ladies would sometimes discuss what they missed most about their lives before moving into the mining settlements. Mom always said her greatest wish when she got back to civilization was for "a full-sized bathtub, in a field of flowers." I don't think she meant a field of wildflowers, either, because there were lots of those kinds of flowers growing on the mountain. Mom's wish was pretty sensible to me, seeing how both of those things were impossible to have where we were at the time. Our baths usually took place in a big, square, galvanized tub. It was okay when you were a kid, because you could fit in comfortably, but I'm sure adults had a difficult time. Mom would heat the water in large kettles on the woodstove, then fill the tub with a few inches of water.

By 1936, the Meridian Mine was closing. Dad explained that it was not profitable to continue working it because the ore body was not as big as had been expected and was of low grade. This meant that we were on the move again. We children did not worry much about leaving our friends behind—we would probably meet them in the next mining town anyway. Usually, the word would get out that another mine was hiring somewhere else and Dad would go along, as the men liked Dad's style of cooking—"meat-and-potato cooking," he called it. Dad said his cooking was more popular than that of the Chinese cooks, who would make the same meal each day of the week, such as chicken on Mondays, stew on Tuesdays, etc., whereas Dad said he never knew what he would cook until it was time to start supper, unless it was Christmas or another special day. At least it gave the miners something to wonder about each day.

And each mine closing gave me a chance to wonder about the new adventures that were on their way for me!

Schoolchildren posing in front of the third Nakusp School (now Nakusp Centennial Building, 92 6th Avenue NW), ca. 1919. Ray and I would finish the 1936 school year here. At right is a partial view of the second school. ARROW LAKES HISTORICAL SOCIETY ARCHIVES, 2003-026-306

8

NAKUSP

I
T WAS APRIL 1936 when we left Camborne for Nakusp. There were still a couple of months of school left in the school year, so once we moved, Ray and I were enrolled in our respective classes. I managed to complete my third grade there, but grade seven proved to be too much for Ray because of the little schooling we had received those years in Camborne. Back then we didn't get a report card; you either passed or failed your grade. There was a lot of pressure to do well, too, because you found out the results after school was out for the summer when the local newspaper posted all the names of the children and whether they passed their grade or failed. They also posted your attendance record for all to see as well. It was a lot more difficult to pull the wool over your parents' eyes back then with any hope of getting away with it.

Our parents rented a house downtown, while Dad went down to Silverton on a job for a short while. He may have been cooking at the Hewitt or Van Roi camp for Mr. Cunningham. I am sure Mom really appreciated the convenience of just walking out the door to reach a store, although I doubt she had any money for anything but the necessities. The house we rented was a two-storey one. It had a bathroom with a real bathtub—however, no field of flowers!

Nakusp is built right on the lakeshore, so Ray and I were able to go swimming. We really enjoyed having the lake to play in. This lake is the Upper Arrow Lake, the same lake that Beaton was built upon, only Beaton was many miles to the northeast of Nakusp. Because we were in Uncle Wat's working territory for the CPR, he would stop in and check on us, sometimes staying a bit for a visit, especially if Dad was home.

All during the Depression, Dad was never out of work for long. In truth, I never knew what that word "depression" really meant when I was a kid. I was twenty-six before I had any understanding of the effects the Depression had on people. I got that understanding from listening to the stories of farmers who had lived through it, telling me what it was like to have no shoes to wear, let alone clothes and toys. I even heard of a family where the children were always hungry, even to the point of eating grass just to put something in their stomachs. God bless the mines and Dad's profession as a cook! We were never hungry at any time, and I never felt I went without. This was probably due to the wisdom of our parents, my mother's prayers, and the generosity of our Slocan and Prairie relatives.

Moms and dads are important to any kid. Ray and I were fortunate to have both be good and kind people, not overly strict, but teaching us the difference between right and wrong and expecting us to follow up on the right—not that we always did, but the good usually won out in the end. Good runs the "norm" in the average family.

Mothers, of course, stayed at home mostly—at least, mothers who had husbands to provide for them and mothers who were satisfied with the provision they got. Families did not compete much for furniture, cars, or unnecessary things at that time. Of course, many of the extras we have today were not invented then. Dad once told me that washing machines were the cause of the Great Depression. Washing machines? He said there was a glut of them, but few had the money to buy them. Well, that is my simplified version of our long conversation, as I trusted that Dad knew best.

We did not stay very long in Nakusp, only about four months. Dad heard that the gold mines at Sheep Creek, six miles east of Salmo, were doing well and were hiring. Dad moved the family back to the Clough Ranch in Slocan while he went ahead to rustle up a job and build us a house in Sheep Creek.

We were always welcome at the ranch, but maybe it was because the relatives knew we would soon be leaving again—no, just kidding, we've always remained a loving family! Ray, Mom, and I did not mind going to stay; we loved being there with our aunt and uncle, and cousins. I suppose we looked upon it as our real home, because it was always the same. The first time I left home on my own, I was very homesick, not for my own home in Nelson, but for the ranch. I guess that was because of its sameness and its stability; it was always the same familiar place, and I was among people I loved.

View of CPR slip and station at Upper Arrow Lake, Nakusp, 1940s. Station agent
Clark walks on wharf at left and Ed Wanstall's delivery truck is left of centre. The Leland
Hotel is above the hillside at centre. ARROW LAKES HISTORICAL SOCIETY ARCHIVES, 2014-003-274

At the ranch, we three families were all pretty comfortable with sharing our space with each other and tried to have a good sense of humour
when someone did something embarrassing or made a comment that was
considered inappropriate.

One such time was when my cousin Fern Cooper, who was about four
years old at the time, was watching my dad washing up one morning and
yelled, "Look, look! Uncle Lee is washing his face all over his head!" It
didn't bother Dad any—he had a good sense of humour. As years went on,
I would tell him about my schemes for curing baldness, but he would just
laugh and say "Don't worry, I tried them all; none of them work." Dad did
have a nice fringe line of hair at the bottom of his hairline. I remember one
day when he was sitting on the porch in Beaton with Mom and me. He was

The *Bonnington* docked at CPR slip next to CPR station, Upper Arrow Lake at Nakusp, 1920s. Photo from postcard produced by the Gowen Sutton Co., Ltd., Vancouver.

waiting for a wagon back to Camborne, and I was standing behind him trying to make little curls in his hair. I asked him why he went to a barber, since had no hair to cut. His response was, "On the contrary, the barber has to earn his money, so he takes a long time to cut what I have." I loved my Dad!

Dad had lost most of his hair when he was eighteen, after a serious case of scarlet fever. Because people associate hair loss with aging, children would frequently ask him about his age, since he still looked young. When asked how old he was, he would reply, "I am as old as my tongue and a little older than my teeth." It took me a bit but I finally figured out what Dad meant: he was born with his tongue but needed time to grow his teeth.

The engine of the train wreck at the Corra Linn Hydroelectric Dam, September 20, 1936.

Ray's friend Gene Hackett on Sheep Creek Road, with Yellowstone Peak in the background, ca. 1938. The road was crude and topped with crushed rock from the mines. Everything travelling on it raised clouds of dust.

SHEEP CREEK

I WAS NINE and Ray was thirteen when we moved to a bustling goldmining town in West Kootenay called Sheep Creek. I think there are as many Sheep Creeks as there are Cambornes in the West Kootenay area. This particular Sheep Creek, however, was about thirty miles south of Nelson, nestled in a valley with a distinct cone-shaped mountain at the valley head. This mountain range was different from the other mountains I had lived among before; here, the mountain peaks were closer together and there were only mountain creeks and small alpine lakes. Missing from the landscape were the larger bodies of water and the whistles of the steamboats. I had a perfect view of a cone-shaped mountain peak, called Yellowstone, from in front of my house and would grow attached to my mountain over the years that Sheep Creek became my home.

I will never forget the day we moved to Sheep Creek from Slocan Valley. We were fortunate to always own a car, even during the Depression. We still had the same Pontiac that we had when we left Sandon, but by then the car had picked up a bad habit of stopping suddenly for no apparent reason—usually while going uphill. Dad would get out of the car and open up one side of the hood, loosen something that was sticking, climb back in the car, and away we would go. Dad had a funny habit that puzzled me whenever we drove up a hill. He would rock back and forth until we got to the top of the hill, then he would stop his rocking. Finally, on this particular trip, as we got to the top of Kosiancic's long steep hill, I could hold my curiosity no longer and I asked him why he did that. His reply was simply that he "was helping the car up the hill." Well, okay, I thought, just as long as we didn't all have to start rocking!

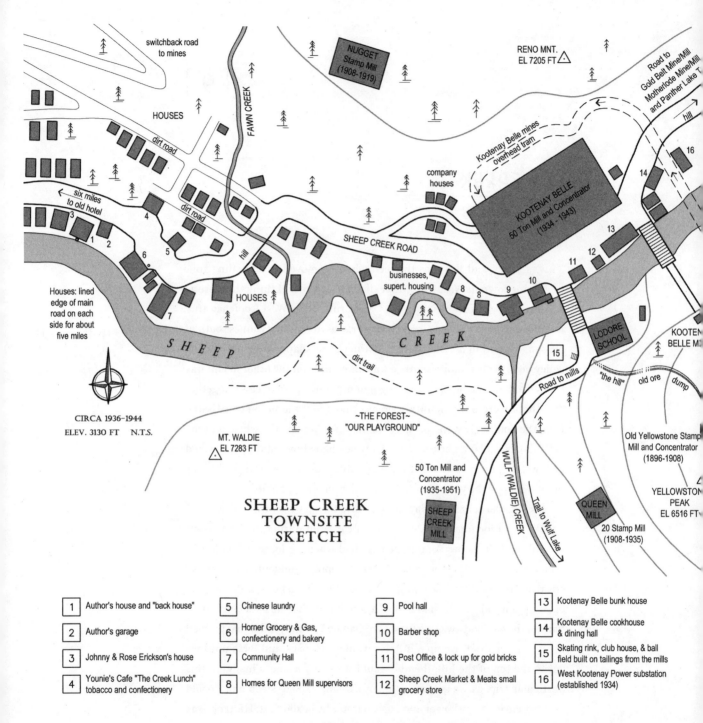

switchback road
to mines

NUGGET
Stamp Mill
(1908-1919)

RENO MNT.
EL 7205 FT

Road to
Gold Belt Mine/Mill
Motherlode Mine/Mill
and Panther Lake T

HOUSES

FAWN CREEK

dirt road

Kootenay Belle mines
overhead tram

company
houses

hill

16

14

KOOTENAY BELLE
50 Ton Mill and
Concentrator
(1934 - 1943)

six miles
to old hotel

dirt road

3

1   2

5

4

6

SHEEP CREEK ROAD

businesses,
supert. housing

13

12

11

8

8

9

10

7

HOUSES

Houses: lined
edge of main
road on each
side for about
five miles

S H E E P

CREEK

15

LODORE
SCHOOL

KOOTEN
BELLE M

dirt trail

Road to mills

"the hill"

old ore

dump

CIRCA 1936-1944
ELEV. 3130 FT   N.T.S.

MT. WALDIE
EL 7283 FT

~THE FOREST~
"OUR PLAYGROUND"

WULF (WALDIE) CREEK

Trail to Wulf Lake

Old Yellowstone Stamp
Mill and Concentrator
(1896-1908)

YELLOWSTON
PEAK
EL 6516 FT

50 Ton Mill and
Concentrator
(1935-1951)

SHEEP
CREEK
MILL

QUEEN
MILL

20 Stamp Mill
(1908-1935)

SHEEP CREEK
TOWNSITE
SKETCH

1	Author's house and "back house"	5	Chinese laundry	9	Pool hall	13	Kootenay Belle bunk house
2	Author's garage	6	Horner Grocery & Gas, confectionery and bakery	10	Barber shop	14	Kootenay Belle cookhouse & dining hall
3	Johnny & Rose Erickson's house	7	Community Hall	11	Post Office & lock up for gold bricks	15	Skating rink, club house, & ball field built on tailings from the mills
4	Younie's Cafe "The Creek Lunch" tobacco and confectionery	8	Homes for Queen Mill supervisors	12	Sheep Creek Market & Meats small grocery store	16	West Kootenay Power substation (established 1934)

Sketch of Sheep Creek townsite, ca. 1940.

Train wreck of a westbound passenger train and an eastbound freight at the Corra Linn Dam on the Kootenay River, just out of Nelson, September 20, 1936. A crowd of people on the opposite hillside gathered to observe the wreck. Photo taken from inside the power plant by Mr. MacDonald. CRANBROOK HISTORY CENTRE ARCHIVES AND THE COLUMBIA BASIN INSTITUTE OF REGIONAL HISTORY, 0382.0001

That day we moved to Sheep Creek was the day of the train wreck at the Corra Linn hydroelectric dam, on the Kootenay River southwest of Nelson. This happened on September 20, 1936. A westbound passenger train (the Kettle Valley Express No. 12) and an eastbound freight train (No. 11) had collided, derailing the engines and tipping an engine and some of the passenger cars over the embankment toward the dam. I used to get

The Kootenay Belle Mill and the mine trestle, Sheep Creek, 1936. The father of my classmate Grace Louise McDonough worked in the offices and was the timekeeper at the Kootenay Belle. The McDonough family lived in one of the company houses near the mill.

carsick, so the stop to see the train wreck scene was a welcome diversion, at least for me. One thing we have to remember about the roads in the Kootenays, in those days, is that they were full of corners. Dad parked the car on the side of the road overlooking the wreck. We got out and took a look, along with a large group of other people already gathering at the edge of the road, taking pictures and talking about the accident. I can still see the scene quite clearly in my mind. There were railcars lying on their sides across the tracks, and the cars looked as if they were right up against the dam. I suppose everyone was afraid that the dam had been damaged. As it was only built in 1932, it was quite new. I do not think anyone was killed or seriously injured, and if there were any casualties, Dad kept them quiet from me, although I never did hear of any later either.

View of Sheep Creek from Yellowstone Mountain, ca. 1936. The Kootenay Belle Mill is on north side of Sheep Creek Road. Across the road from the mill is (*L-R*) Thos Jadro's pool hall and barber shop, the bridge, the post office, Sheep Creek Market, and Kootenay Belle bunkhouse. Note the woman hanging out laundry across Sheep Creek by the backhouse. Across the bridge is the Lodore School and the road leading to the Queen Mill and mine.

DAD'S FIRST JOB in Sheep Creek was cooking for the men from the Kootenay Belle Mine. The bunkhouse and cookhouse were along the side of the road and near the mine's crusher mill, which was very close to being part of the townsite of Sheep Creek.

Dad had built us a house about a mile or so down the road from the mill while we were waiting for him to collect us from the ranch. It was between the creek and the road above the creek bank, Sheep Creek Road, the main street in town. The house had three little rooms: a living room/kitchen and two small bedrooms. Mom and Dad slept in one bedroom, I

Our house and garage in Sheep Creek, September 1938. We had
electricity but no indoor plumbing. *L–R*: Dad, the author, Aunt Bertha,
cousin Beth, Mom, Ray, and cousin Hughie, with his toy six-shooter.

Mom and Dad's second car, a dark-green 1934 Chevrolet Deluxe Master
sedan, Sheep Creek, 1937. *L–R*: Lee and Jennie Hall, Ida Lieb, and Aunt Grace.
Younie's Café (also known as the Creek Lunch Café) is in the background.

slept in the other, and Ray slept on the Winnipeg in the living room until Dad could build on another room, which became his and Mom's new bedroom, and Ray took over their old one—finally, for the first time ever, his own bedroom.

The kitchen stove was our only source of heat. I had never heard of such a thing as insulation in walls and ceilings. Some people used crumpled newspapers to fill the cracks in the walls, or sawdust, which I suppose acted as some kind of insulation, or at least kept the wind from blowing through the house. In the winter, we always went to bed with a hot water bottle and, of course, the quilts, stuffed with real sheep's wool, that Mom had made for each bed. Sometime later, Dad built a garage for our car as well. He eventually sold the Pontiac and bought a dark-green 1934 Chevrolet Deluxe Master sedan.

The outdoors was the place to get rid of human waste if you lived where there was no indoor running water. And, if it was too cold or too dark to go outdoors, the solution was the chamber pot. Even today, both methods are used in certain cases. The outhouse, or backhouse as we used to call it, was always located out back of the house. It was basically a pit dug in the ground with a windowless, sturdy privacy shed built around it. The seat was a wooden board with a hole cut in the centre, large enough to be comfortable but small enough so that you couldn't fall through. A friend once asked me, "What did you use when you had no toilet paper?" The answer was simple: the Eaton's catalogue! Well, only after Christmas had passed. She was quite shocked. It was not really a pleasant option, especially with the glossy pages. Actually, if the future is going to become less civilized, I really hope the last thing to go will be toilet tissue. These days, you can buy a little folding seat to use for that same purpose while camping or hiking. They look comfortable, and there are always thimbleberry bushes within arm's reach. You may be laughing, but this unpleasantness is no laughing matter at all, especially to an owner who did not build the backhouse strong enough to withstand the showing off of four or five teenage boys on Halloween night. Of course, the moving or tipping over of the privacy shed was supposed to be humorous—at least to the kids who did it.

The townsite of Sheep Creek was located at the confluence of Sheep and Wulf (Waldie) creeks. The houses and businesses were shoehorned into the valley among the existing mills, bunkhouses, and cookhouses of the Sheep Creek mining camps. There were four mills in operation at that time: Queen, Kootenay Belle, Gold Belt, and Motherlode. The Queen and

Kootenay Belle mills were part of the town, while the Gold Belt Mill was a little farther up the road from the Kootenay Belle. The Motherlode mill was located the farthest up the road, past all the other mills and away from the town's business area. I remember the assayers would bring the gold bricks to the post office, where they would lock up the bricks until the gold could be couriered to the CPR and then to the Consolidated Mining and Smelting Company (Cominco) in Trail. There was no rail line to Sheep Creek.

At the height of the town's activity, the population was about twelve hundred people, mostly miners with their families, as well as a good number of young men hailing from other places coming to work in the mines. The whole town stretched along each side of Sheep Creek Road, above the creek, for probably four or five miles. By 1941 there were well over a hundred houses, built next to each other with very little yard space on either side. Most of the people coming into Sheep Creek were of northern European descent, mainly Swedish, Norwegians, and some Germans. There were a few Chinese men in town who ran a Chinese laundry and a bathhouse; the men living in the bunkhouses used their services. The only place I had ever seen any Chinese people prior to Sheep Creek was downtown in Nelson; I never saw a Chinese woman.

I didn't really pay attention to the reasons why we moved so much when I was a kid. To me, it was simply because one mine ran out of silver or gold and another new one opened. I was content following my family and just being an adventuresome kid. It wasn't until I was a teenager that I started to understand that most mines hadn't run out of silver or gold; instead, they usually closed because the mine was no longer profitable enough for the mining companies to keep them open.

A schoolmate of mine, Bill Cartwright, and his family were already living in Sheep Creek when our family arrived. In a letter to me years later, Bill recounted how the increased value of gold during the Depression resulted in several new and refurbished mining operations opening up in Sheep Creek during the 1930s. He also remembered the numerous summer "relief camps" bordering the main road to Sheep Creek, where young men lived and did the roadwork for their food, tobacco, and a few cents a day. It was these men from the government relief camps who gradually improved the road safety and travel time to Nelson. How grateful I am to them!

I remember that the roads were dusty in the summer and snowy in the winter. Sheep Creek was about an hour away from Nelson, less than thirty-five miles by car. The road from Ymir toward Salmo was full of

The houses of Sheep Creek were built next to each other, with little yard space on either side, ca. 1937. Schoolmate Judy Bremner holds her little dog, Prince, and stands beside a neighbour.

The new houses built across the road from author's house, Sheep Creek, September 1, 1939. The population more than doubled in just one year.

Grading the road from Salmo to Nelson, 1938.

The heavy snow would act like insulation. Our garage and
house are on the left and neighbour Johnny (Jens) and Rose
Erickson's house is on the right. Sheep Creek, 1938.

Horner's Grocery and Gas, just up from our house. Sheep Creek, ca. 1938.

corners and I would get carsick when we travelled on it, although Ray did not. Travelling in winter was sometimes precarious. From an early age, we were prepared for an unscheduled pileup into a snowbank, or a sudden snowslide, an accident, a rock slide, or having the car just slide off the road because of a soft shoulder. More than once during winter, I remember Dad not making a corner and then sliding headfirst (or car-nose first) into a snowbank. Never to worry, Dad carried a snow shovel and some dirt to put under the tires for traction to help get us back on our way.

One winter morning, on our trip to town, on the part of the road between Salmo and Ymir, a car coming around a corner from the opposite direction hit our car; I was sitting behind Dad. Dad had turned the steering wheel hard, but our vehicle went straight anyway, right into a snowbank. Lucky for us, the snowbank on the outside edge of the road held solid and stopped us from going over the embankment. We were all a bit shook up, but no one was seriously hurt. Our car needed some repairs, though.

At one time, the road to Nelson used to go through the settlement named Porto Rico Siding, which once had a prosperous gold and copper mine, then later a lumberyard and sawmill. The railways discontinued use of the siding; afterward, the Porto Rico–Ymir traffic was rerouted

Aunt Grace visiting from Spooner, Saskatchewan, summer 1939. In the background are houses and Younie's Creek Lunch Café. Across Sheep Creek Road was Horner's Gas and Grocery and the Community Hall. This photo was taken from in front of our house.

Yellowstone Peak, the gas pumps of Horner's Gas and Grocery, and the Community Hall to the far right, summer 1938. Annie Karchie, the author, and Eva Karchie.

to the current Nelson–Nelway Highway. By 1941, the settlement had been abandoned.

Our family lived in Sheep Creek longer than anywhere else before, about seven years; I myself lived there about five and a half years (from grades four to nine). Mom and Dad remained there for two more years, while I boarded in Nelson during the week for high school and came home for the weekend. As Sheep Creek grew, the roads from Salmo to Nelson improved, especially when the government built a long, straight stretch from Salmo to the railway crossing. I always felt that I grew up along with the road from Salmo to Nelson, as it took so long for the government to construct it. As I remember, the base of the road was made of silica rock hauled from several of the Sheep Creek mine dumps.

ONE OF THE things about living in a valley with high mountains on either side is the lack of wind. I don't remember at any time being particularly cold. The heavy snow acted as insulation, I suppose. But when we went to

In 1938 the Big Little Book series became the Better
Little Book series. Flash Gordon was my hero.

Nelson in the winter, it was another story. That whistling west wind would come sweeping up Baker Street from the West Arm of Kootenay Lake and the train station like a cold banshee. I was glad Grandma lived in the Fairview part of Nelson; the wind didn't seem to be as strong there. But I could not wait to head back to Sheep Creek to get out of it.

Most Saturdays were taken up with travelling to Nelson for shopping and a visit with Grandpa and Grandma Hall. For shopping in Sheep Creek, there was the Sheep Creek Market, a small tobacco and general market across the creek from the school, and the two stores near our house, Horner's general gas-and-grocery store and a small convenience store in Younie's Café. My personal shopping was always done at Woolworth's, the five-and-dime store (locally we called it "the fifteen-cents store"). This is where I bought my Big Little Books and Better Little Books. I paid ten cents apiece for them.

I loved to read, sometimes as many as eight hours in a day; the subjects were varied. Dad loved to read too. Perhaps his appreciation for books and information rubbed off on me. I'm sure Dad never had an opportunity to pursue schooling past grade nine, so he welcomed the Frontier College reading tents that would come to some of the mining and relief camps.

Each tent was fully stocked with books and a volunteer teacher who was typically a university student. The college's mission was to bring education and enlightenment to the labourers in remote areas, even if it was just helping them learn how to read and write. Dad liked the library where he could check out real classical novels to read, instead of just the newspaper. I would often boast to Dad how many pages I could read in a day. One winter day, Dad challenged me to a reading match to see who could read the most number of pages in a week. Each day we would take turns reading the book for a set equal amount time, and then mark our page where we left off. I don't think we settled on a prize; it was probably just that the winner would have bragging rights. I also don't remember the book we read, but I do recall that Dad won by a landslide, because I never told him that I could out-read him again after that.

One of my passions in my preteen years was reading titles in the Big Little Book series, of which I bought many. The books were small and bulky, and made of inexpensive paper with a coloured hardboard cover. The left-hand pages contained the story, and a drawing in black and white was on every opposing page. It was the drawings that I liked best. They were good, and I would practise my drawing skills by copying them. The back cover listed "The Best of the Better Little Books," *Mickey Mouse, Donald Duck, The Lone Ranger, Dick Tracey the Detective, Tom Mix, Buck Jones, Tarzan of the Apes, Little Orphan Annie, Dan Dunn, Secret Operative 48, King of the Royal Mounted*, and on and on. Out of all of the books, Flash Gordon was my hero, with Dale Arden as his sweetheart. I have The Better Little Book *Flash Gordon and the Perils of Mongo* in front of me at the moment. I think I will read it again—all 424 pages! I don't know how many hero adventure stories I have read in my life, but the plots never change: It's always good against evil, the ladies are all dressed up as sexy as they were when I was a kid, the bad guys are ugly, the heroes are gorgeous, and the power-hungry kill anyone who gets in their way, other than the hero and his lady. And guess who wins? Thank goodness, it's always the good guys!

We often stayed late in Nelson on a Saturday to catch a seven o'clock movie. The doorman at the Civic Theatre was cute, which I came to appreciate later in life. One evening, when I was about thirteen, Grace Tonkin, my friend from Sheep Creek, accompanied me to a movie. When we passed by this particular doorman, I remarked that "he sure is cute." Grace

My first real crush, Jimmy (James Kenneth) Younie, in the navy, ca. 1942.

replied, "Oh, I know him, he already has a girlfriend," to which I sighed, "Okay," and promptly forgot him. Little did I know at that time, this cute doorman and Boy Scout, Freddie Stainton, would go off to fight the war in Europe, though just like the plot in the stories, it turned out all right, because six years later, after he returned from the war, I married him.

We were not brought up on movies the way the world is today. The only movies in Sheep Creek were shown by a man who rented the community hall and set it up as a theatre to show the community his homemade black-and-white film reel. I don't remember what the film was about, but

One of our favourite places to hang out was on the steps of Younie's Café. *L-R*: Grace Louise McDonough, Hannah (she was new), and Bertha Boyer. Jimmy's dog Chief is asleep on the steps, and his little brother Peter sits behind the girls on the deck. Sheep Creek, 1940.

I suspect the content (like a lot of home movies) was about some of his recent travels.

The community hall was the only building to rent for a special occasion or to hold a community event. The hall was across the road, kitty-corner to Mrs. Younie's Café, which was about a block or so up the road from our home. The Horner's general gas-and-grocery was between our house and the hall. These buildings were on the main road up to the mills. Sometimes dances and concerts where held in the hall. We had live music in those days for our dances, provided by an orchestra that came from Salmo.

As it was for most teenagers, it was an awkward time in our young lives for communication with the opposite sex, especially when it came to dancing. One of the older girls, Florence MacIntyre, taught us girls about dancing, but I don't know if the boys were taught at all. The girls would sit along the wall on one side of the hall, while the boys stood around or sat along the wall on the other side. I liked Jimmy Younie and I very much wanted him to dance with me; he was the boy I had my first real crush on. The other boys, too afraid to approach any of the girls, wanted Jimmy to go first and ask me to dance. Well, he finally mustered up the courage, but by this time I had become so shy that I said no. Wrong answer! Jimmy was now so doubly embarrassed and shy that he walked back to the other side of the hall with his head hung low. I felt awful, too. I had missed my chance! Jimmy was a good pal, though, even after I embarrassed him. When he got older, he enlisted in the navy and sent me a picture of himself on his ship. He was still cute as ever!

Two of our favourite places to hang out were on the front steps of Mrs. Younie's Café, which Jimmy's mom owned, and Horner's Confectionery, owned by the parents of our pal Bill Horner. Younie's Café, also called the Creek Lunch Counter, sold tobacco and confectionery, and had a lunch counter with a pool room and barbershop downstairs. Ma Younie, as we all called her, also had a jukebox at the lunch counter that we sometimes listened to, but mostly we liked to hang out on the front-porch steps and talk about things important to us kids as we watched the townspeople go by. There was a good group of us kids in Sheep Creek, enough to make games like kick-the-can and hide-and-seek more exciting and fun.

Our annual Christmas concert was what every child waited for. It was held in our community hall. It was the biggest yearly event, so the whole town would turn out. (That was the one nice thing about having the mills right in town: Dad was able to come home every night and even attend special events.) I remember the big stage and the huge Christmas tree that the miners would cut from the forest and put up to decorate. The concert was composed of the usual skits, recitations, and instrumentals. After the concert came Santa Claus, with a present for each child. All of the children were, of course, very excited by it all, as they still are today. The kids would open up the presents right, left, and centre; you only hoped you had the right one when you got home. The evening would be capped off with cookies and soft drinks.

One year, Ray, who was one of the older children, received a box camera, film, and all the equipment for developing film and printing his own photos. I'm sorry to admit that I don't remember what I received each year—it was usually a game, or mitts and a cap; I had outgrown dolls already. Santa usually gave out several of the same type of gift to the

The boys hanging out at Younie's Café, ca. 1939. *L–R*: Jimmy Younie, Ray Hall, Jim McDonough, Bud McIntyre, Don Lane, Roy Asplund, Peter Younie.

different age groups of children. This explains why, one year, there seemed to be several pictures in our family album of teenagers taking pictures of other teenagers. I never asked, nor was I ever told directly, but I believe our Santa gifts came from the generosity of the mining companies, which also paid for the Christmas concert and refreshments. It had been a few years since Betty Baines and I had made that all-important decision to not question our parents about the identity of Santa Claus while in Camborne. Perhaps the reason that Santa's gifts didn't leave a lasting impression on me, just a few years later, was that I was growing up and realizing that the true gift and magic of Christmas was being able to be with the ones you love.

I can't remember ever having a birthday party as a child, or, for that matter, ever attending anyone else's. Ray's and my birthdays were in February, which in BC was still in the winter. I am sure that our parents gave us a gift, probably clothing, as these were the Depression days. But I wonder why I don't remember having birthday parties, or at least going

Annie Cavalier and the author. The aviator hat and goggles were one of the Christmas concert gifts that many of us kids received from Santa. Sheep Creek, ca. 1937.

to one. Did birthday parties just become popular later, or were they just for grownups? Maybe only rich people gave their children birthday parties. During my teen years, our parents did give us each a birthday gift and certainly we always exchanged gifts at Christmastime with relatives, but that was about it for presents. Instead, we celebrated special days with a family dinner, and if it was a birthday, the birthday girl or boy would get to choose the menu and dessert, which usually was their favourite food.

Winter was my favourite season, particularly because of the sports. I loved the deep snow and any chance to go sleigh riding, skiing, and skating on the outdoor rink. The first fall of snow, with its large lacy flakes, always excited me and sent me asking Mom, "Where's my snowsuit?" In the winter, I practically lived in my blue snowsuit. While other girls could be seen wearing their dresses and heavy winter coats, I could be seen in my blue snowsuit, aviator hat, and goggles, until I got a little older; then I could be seen wearing my more stylish powder-blue snowsuit. It was probably one I designed, and which Mom lovingly sewed for me. The

Author standing on the front porch of the Lodore School wearing the powder-blue snowsuit her Mom sewed for her. The porch was part of the additions to the building as the school grew, as seen in the large class photo (p.136). Sheep Creek, 1941.

aviator hat and goggles were one of the Christmas concert Santa gifts that many of us kids received one year. I believe this was Christmas of 1936 or maybe 1937. They were a popular gift that year because of Amelia Earhart making world news with her plans to fly around the world in 1937. She would have been the first woman to make the longest global flight in aviator history, but sadly, near the end of her trip, she and her plane disappeared somewhere east of New Guinea near a tiny island named Howland. Amelia and her plane were never found, but I still liked to wear the hat and goggles because we both were adventurers.

I loved to go sleigh riding. We used the open road for our runs, since there were few vehicles to compete with. Of course, there were lots of hills to slide on, too. On one of my sleigh rides, something happened that made me again leery of German shepherd dogs; I had not forgotten my earlier experience with the Evans dog in Beaton. This particular dog belonged to one of the boys on another sleigh in front of me. Several of us kids would rope our sleighs together, and once my sleigh was on the tail end. With all the noise and yelling, the dog got excited, grabbed my pant leg, and pulled me off my sleigh. Needless to say, my yells outshouted the rest, and I grabbed my sleigh and headed for home.

Our school in Sheep Creek was built next to an old mine dump, the waste (called tailings) left over from the long-gone Yellowstone Mill. The dump was not very wide, but it was very steep. At that time the Coca-Cola Company used to advertise on very large metal signs, about the size of a two-person toboggan. Somehow, I got hold of one of these signs and decided it was just the right size to use as a toboggan to slide down that particular dump, as the dump was covered in deep snow. I told the rest of the kids what I planned to do, and they all came out to watch the show—including my dad, from the Kootenay Belle cookhouse, who I did not know was watching me at the time. I took my tin toboggan and climbed to the top of the hill, bent up the front into a curl, and sat on it for about two seconds. Instantly, the tin sign started to slide on the dry snow. I fell off the sign, it flew into the air, and I tumbled head over heels right to the bottom of the dump, where my "toboggan" was waiting for me. Oh well, one more lesson learned. Dad didn't say a word.

In hindsight, I should have asked one of the Scandinavian men from the Kootenay Belle where Dad was working to give me some tips ahead of time. One of the men had built a Swedish sleigh, a kicksled. It looked like a tall chair attached to two skis. The sledder would stand on the back of one ski, and while holding onto a handle bar attached to the back of the chair, he would kick his other foot back on the ground and propel the sled forward. The sled was very pliable and easily steered whichever way the sledder moved his body and twisted the handle bar. There was a short hill from the Kootenay Belle cookhouse to the store near the bridge, where this man would take his sleigh to buy hardtack and other items, then use his sleigh to carry the items back to his bunkhouse. Hardtack, or knacker-brod, is a large round thin rye-crisp cracker that has a hole in its centre. It is very delicious and was a popular treat for the Swedish and Norwegian miners. Dad would often bake it for the Kootenay Belle miners to give them a taste of home.

Ray and I both had skis. One of the Scandinavian miners built Ray a pair of jumping skis. I don't remember that he ever became very accomplished with them, as they were very wide and heavy. Ray and I usually skied with a group of other kids on the side roads that led up both sides of the valley to other mine sites. Skiing was fun, but my real love was skating.

I learned to skate young. I don't remember how old I was, but my first skates were strapped onto my rubbers. I don't think the skates had boots on them then, at least, mine didn't, but we all wore overshoes—everyone, even dads. I spent as much time skating as I could. As I got older, I played on a girls' hockey team, but on booted skates. We played games against the Salmo girls' hockey team in Salmo, because they had an indoor rink. I was not a great player. I played left wing, but I was not a great player. I used to get chastised for always getting excited and being offside, ahead of the centre player and the other wing. But I still loved to skate!

The townspeople had built a good-sized skating rink for the Sheep Creek community, which doubled as a ball park in the summer. There was not a large enough area of levelled ground anywhere to have a rink or playing field, so the community levelled out the old Yellowstone Mill tailings pond below our school to make one. The tailings created a good base for the rink as the soil was bad and nothing, not even weeds, would grow there. The rink was fancy—it even had a clubhouse and outdoor lights for evening skating. We never paid to use the ball park or the rink—it was always available for us kids.

One particular Saturday, I was at the rink with my friends when I got to wondering how fast I could skate around the inner perimeter of it. I asked my friends to time me while I skated once around the rink. I remember gliding up to them at the conclusion of my run and calling out, "How long?" The next thing I remember was waking up in the shack with everyone hovering over me. Yup—I had fallen on the ice and knocked myself out. But I don't recall even having a headache.

I do remember another skating incident. During a hockey game I was playing in, I was hit across the nose with an opponent's stick. Dr. Morrison came to the house on his way back to Nelson to assess the damage the stick had done to my poor nose. "Yes," he said, "The nose does look broken, but I can't do a thing about it." I have always wondered if I would have had a nice, straight nose had it not been for that accident.

There were only two bridges in town that crossed the creek. One led to the Kootenay Belle mines, the other to our school, called Lodore School, the ice rink/ball field, and the Queen Mill. Our school was up near the mills, right by the bridge. We understood that the name of our school was chosen by the school inspector, who came from Nelson frequently to inspect the school. The one-roomed school later grew to be a two-roomed, then a three-roomed one, with grades one to nine. Our teachers were Mr. Charles Unsworth (also the principal), Miss Edna McKenzie, and Miss Leslie Fraser. I knew Miss McKenzie, as she had been a Sunday school

The woodshed behind Lodore School, 1937. Annie and Mary Cavalier and
Miss Fraser stand at the left, and Bobby Hallbauer is on the right far. The
Cavalier family moved away from Sheep Creek the summer of 1938.

Sheep Creek Lodore School, 1938–39, Ray's graduating year. As the town grew, our one-room
school went under construction twice, expanding to a three-room school with grades
one to nine. The right side of the building shows evidence of new construction.

L–R, back row: 1-Bill Horner, 2-brother to 23, 3-Bob Hallbauer, 4-Bill Cartwright,
5-Fred Boyer, 6-Brian Mondini, 7-unknown, 8-Roy Asplund, 9-Ray Hall, 10-Jim McDonough,
11-Don Lane, 12-Bud McIntyre, 13-Roy Lindblad, 14-Billy Bell. *Third row:* 15-Bertha Boyer,
16-Grace Louise McDonough, 17- Shirley Hall (author), 18-Judy Bremner, 19-Annie Karchie,
20-Florence MacIntyre, 21-Eva Karchie, 22-Lila Melbie, 23-sister to 2, 24-unknown, 25/26-sisters,
27-unknown. *Second row:* 28–33-unknown, 34-Peter Younie, 35-Leslie Fraser (teacher),
36-Charles Unsworth (principal, teacher), 37-Edna McKenzie (teacher), 38-Bob Duncan,
39-Jimmy Duncan, 40-Ruth Olsen, 41-Caroline Olsen, 42-unknown, 43-Rosie Karchie,
44-unknown (Rosie's best friend), 45-unknown, 46-Cartwright, 47-unknown.
First row: 48–50-unknown, 51-Ron MacIntyre, 52-unknown, 53-Lillian Cartwright,
54–58-unknown, 59-Alvina Boyer, 60-Norman Cosnett, 61-Louis Ponti,
62-Bob McNab, 63/64-unknown, 65/66-twin sisters, 67-unknown.

student at the Christian Science church in Nelson that I had sometimes attended. Miss Fraser was the fifth daughter of the seven girls of the Fraser family of Fraser Landing. (Fraser Landing used to be the west terminal of the main Kootenay Lake ferry—the *Nasookin*, from 1931 to 1947, until the *Anscomb* took over her run in the summer of 1947 at the newly built ferry landing in Balfour. The site of Fraser Landing is along the Fraser Narrows at the end of Heuston Road in Balfour.)

Bobby Hallbauer was one of my schoolmates. Our fathers worked together at the Queen Mill up past our school after my Dad quit cooking for the Kootenay Belle. Bobby was three years younger than me, and so we mostly hung out with different kids unless we were playing games for which it was more fun to involve a larger group of kids. He was more interested in what the older boys were doing anyway and would ask them sometimes if he could tag along. Bobby was a nice kid; Ray, who was seven years older, looked out for him. Who could have guessed back then that Bobby would grow up to later become president of Cominco, the smelter in Trail? He was inducted into the Canadian Mining Hall of Fame in 1996 for his contribution to the development of the Canadian mining industry.

MR. UNSWORTH AND I used to tangle quite often. Things were different back then in schools, and kids were punished for many things. I was a great line writer (a lighter type of punishment), and if that didn't work out, there was always the dreaded strap. One time, Mr. Unsworth gave me the sentence, "The longest way around is the shortest way home," to write out one hundred times. This was my punishment for frog jumping over the school seats at recess. Mr. Unsworth did not like students doing this, so every time he caught me jumping over the seats, I would get a larger number of lines to write, and if I did not write them all out, he would keep adding on more. Maybe he thought he was only trying to make a lady out of me.

In those days, teachers were allowed to strap students on their palms, but not on the wrists, for bad behaviour. Mr. Unsworth's strap was a piece of belting from a mill, with rubber on one side and rough, hard cloth on the other. We were given our choice as to which side we would prefer: if you took the rubber side, it stung badly, while the cloth side did not hurt as much—unless he got you up on the wrist—but it left bad bruises. Needless to say, I had a number of bruises. My only comfort was that I was not the

Lodore school group hiking up to Panther Lake, 1939.
L-R: Mr. Unsworth, Ray Hall, Elizabeth (Lizzie) Mears, Jim McDonough,
Don Lane, the author, Grace Louise McDonough, Bob McNab.

Ray took this photo on a class day hike to Panther Lake, above Sheep
Creek, and developed the photo himself, ca. 1938. The equipment he used
was the Christmas gift he received at the community Christmas party.

only one. One day, Ray and Jimmy McDonough stole the strap, chopped
it up with an axe, and threw it into the creek. My heroes! There was only
one problem; I was the first one to get into trouble after they took that
brave action. So what did the teacher do? Mr. Unsworth was so mad that
he could not find his strap that he sent me home. This did not sit well with
Dad, as you might suppose. I told Dad and Mom my story (that I really was
innocent this time, honest!) and Dad said I was not to go back to school.

After two days had passed, Dad told Ray to tell the teacher to come and see him. Mr. Unsworth showed up at the house that evening. After some discussion, he finally listened to my side of the story, and the matter was settled. I was also relieved of Mr. Unsworth's punishment of writing lines, as Dad told him that writing out sentences was rather fruitless. I still remember that particular sentence, though, even if I never did write out all two thousand lines I had supposedly earned. I am sure that if I had, I would have used up all the paper in the school. I went back to school the next day. I do not remember whether Mr. Unsworth ever got another strap or not, but if he did, he never used it on Ray or me again.

I was never really sure what Mr. Unsworth thought of me. Possibly this was his first time overseeing this many students. He may have felt he was personally responsible for each of us and so always needed to show his authority. I know he was very upset when he saw me pitching softball for the ladies' team when I was fourteen. The young mothers in town had a ball team, but none of them could pitch. They let me play, as I could pitch the ball a little. I was in grade nine at the time, but Mr. Unsworth said I was too young to be playing with them. I don't know what he thought they were going to teach me!

Most of the hiking we did was typically day hikes for school. We would have the choice between hiking to Panther Lake or Wulf (Waldie) Lake. They were both about the same distance from town and started out on the same main trail, near the Gold Belt Mine's mill. I preferred to go to Panther Lake, because I thought it was the prettier of the two, but it didn't really matter, as these class trips always provided some valuable lesson.

I remember that on one hike, we took with us some cans of pork and beans. Our intent was to build a fire and eat a hot lunch. This proved to be a challenge, though, as no one had remembered to bring a can opener. Mr. Unsworth had an axe with him, so we used that to open up the cans of beans; however, there was still another problem to solve. No student had remembered to bring any matches to start a campfire. For some reason, we students had thought that Mr. Unsworth smoked cigarettes, so we assumed that he would have matches with him. To our surprise, we found out that he didn't smoke, and that he didn't remember to bring any matches either. In the end, we ate our pork and beans cold. As was often the case in our classroom hikes, we learned how to find solutions to sometimes unique problems, and also about the dangers of making

I taught myself to draw from comic strips and the Big Little books.
Collage of drawings done in pen and ink and pencil, all drawn in 1946.

assumptions about people, places, and things. For instance, someone once gave Ray a new hatchet, making the assumption that he actually knew how to use one. He took the hatchet on a hike with us to Panther Lake. Then, while steadying a log with his foot, he took one swing with it and put the hatchet right through the toe of his boot. Luckily, the axe missed all of his toes.

I was about nine when I took a real interest in drawing, but my interest in pictures probably started when I was small. One of the ways Mom would entertain me was by taking a coloured picture and putting it on the floor. I would lie down on my tummy beside it and study the picture for hours. As I got older, I would spend many hours in the snowy winter evenings at the kitchen table, drawing to my heart's content. I taught myself to draw from comic strips and the Big Little books. I merely copied what I saw—after all, the pictures were just simple line drawings. I couldn't stand to see an empty, clean piece of crisp, white paper without wanting to draw something on it, but I was running out of paper. Finally, I discovered the local paper boy, who had sheets of clean newsprint, which he used for wrapping the bundles of the *Nelson Daily News* and the *Toronto Star* to keep them clean during transit. I asked the paper boy to save the newsprint for me, and then I would make the sheets of paper into drawing booklets. My first models were in the funnies: Maggie and Jiggs, Betty Boop, Blondie, and Li'l Abner. As I got better, I started drawing portraits, which have remained my favourite choice of drawing or painting to create.

THOUGH NOVEMBER 11 keeps coming around every year, I never experience that day without remembering one I spent in Sheep Creek. It must have been 1938, as the Second World War had not yet begun. I did not have a watch, so I was not sure of the time, but I did know it was Remembrance Day; because Dad had been in the First World War, we especially observed that day. There was snow on the road, and I was all alone, presumably going from Grace Louise's house to my own, or vice versa. It had snowed earlier that morning, but the snow on the road was packed enough that I could use my sleigh. There was one spot on the road, close to where the school bridge crossed the creek, where you could look over Sheep Creek and see the skating rink and the Queen Mill. I had stopped there for a moment to take a look. Suddenly, the whistle from the Queen Mill began to blow, followed by the Kootenay Belle and Gold Belt mills, signalling the start of the three minutes of silence. I dutifully sat quietly on my sleigh for my three minutes until the whistles gave a short blast signalling the end of the silence. However, the three minutes of silence seemed to last a little longer for me in my white world.

In the summer, my playmates and I would play in the woods across the creek that ran down the valley. There were fairy bowers and rocks with moss for us to sit on. We girls were queens and princesses on our thrones of soft, green moss. We loved all the wildflowers and ferns; the lady's slippers were so delicate and lovely. There were also yellow slide lilies, trilliums, and stars of Bethlehem, and even a small gurgling stream that added to the beauty. (Honest!) The boys used to play separately from us in the same area, only they were doing whatever it is that boys do, like play-fighting, boxing, fishing, and taking photos, or picking through piles of old mining junk.

ONE OF MY first lessons in vanity came when I turned thirteen and was told to look after my own hair. By this time, the mining town had grown to roughly a thousand residents, one of whom was a hairdresser with a beauty shop. We were having a school concert, and this particular year all the girls were privileged to have their hair done professionally. The hairdresser, Virginia McMillan, was a young woman who knew her job.

She taught all of us girls how we should wear our hair to look the most becoming. I listened to her, and even today, I still follow her advice. I don't remember who cut my and Ray's hair in the early days, but it was probably Mom or Dad. Ray went to one of the barbers in town when we got older. There were two barber shops, one downstairs in Younie's Café and one by the pool hall near the bridge by the school. I think most of the boys had Mr. Cohen, who was the barber at Younie's Café, cut their hair. He was a nice man and got quite some laughs out of us kids. Grace Louise's mom used to send her to the barber by the pool hall to have her hair cut, much to Grace's disgust. I'm not sure why she was so upset, her hair always looked good to me.

As children who lived surrounded by the forest, we encountered a problem with a bug called a wood tick. The tick would get in our hair and embed its head into our skin if we didn't catch them right away, but we had no fear of them. Grace Louise, Judy, and I would go up the mountain in late March when the snow had melted and find wood ticks all over the ground where they had hatched. We would each find two ticks (in case we lost one on the way down the mountain) and put them in an empty match box to take back to the school. Before class started and during recess, we would race the bugs against each other. I think the teacher finally put a stop to this sport.

We were taught that you never pulled a tick from the flesh of a person or animal, because the body would break off and the head would remain embedded. What we did was use a hot needle and touched the rear of the tick; that way the bug would back out on its own and bring its head with it. Ticks are bloodsuckers and would swell to the size of a pea or larger after feeding. As children do (at least, we did), we killed them by dropping them onto a hot stove, where they would promptly burst. Wood ticks were hard to kill because of the flat shape of their body; and because they were only about an eighth of an inch long and very stealthy, you were seldom aware of their presence on your flesh. I once took one off Mom's back that was swollen to twice its size, and she never felt it at all; she had thought it was some sort of scab.

Mom was hard of hearing and could not hear us when we answered her calls, so she used a whistle to call us to ensure we would hear her. Ray and I would hear the whistle but were loath to leave our playing. Ray, being the oldest, would always inform me, "Mom is calling you!" To which I would answer, "No! She wants you!" He would reply, "Well, then, you go

Photos of the way we played. *L–R, top to bottom:*

L–R: Bud McIntyre and Roy Asplund going fishing. Sheep Creek.

L–R: a friend, Ray, Gus (wearing hat), Banjo, Frank. Sunday afternoon in Sheep Creek.

Boys picking through dirt and piles of old mining junk. Sheep Creek.

The way we played house: Judy Bremner, behind her house in Sheep Creek, 1937.

Sunday afternoon with the gang. Freddie Thompson is taking a picture of us girls.
L–R: Hannah, Ruth, Bertha Boyer, the author, Grace Louise McDonough,
Florence MacIntyre, Eva Karchie. Sheep Creek, 1940.

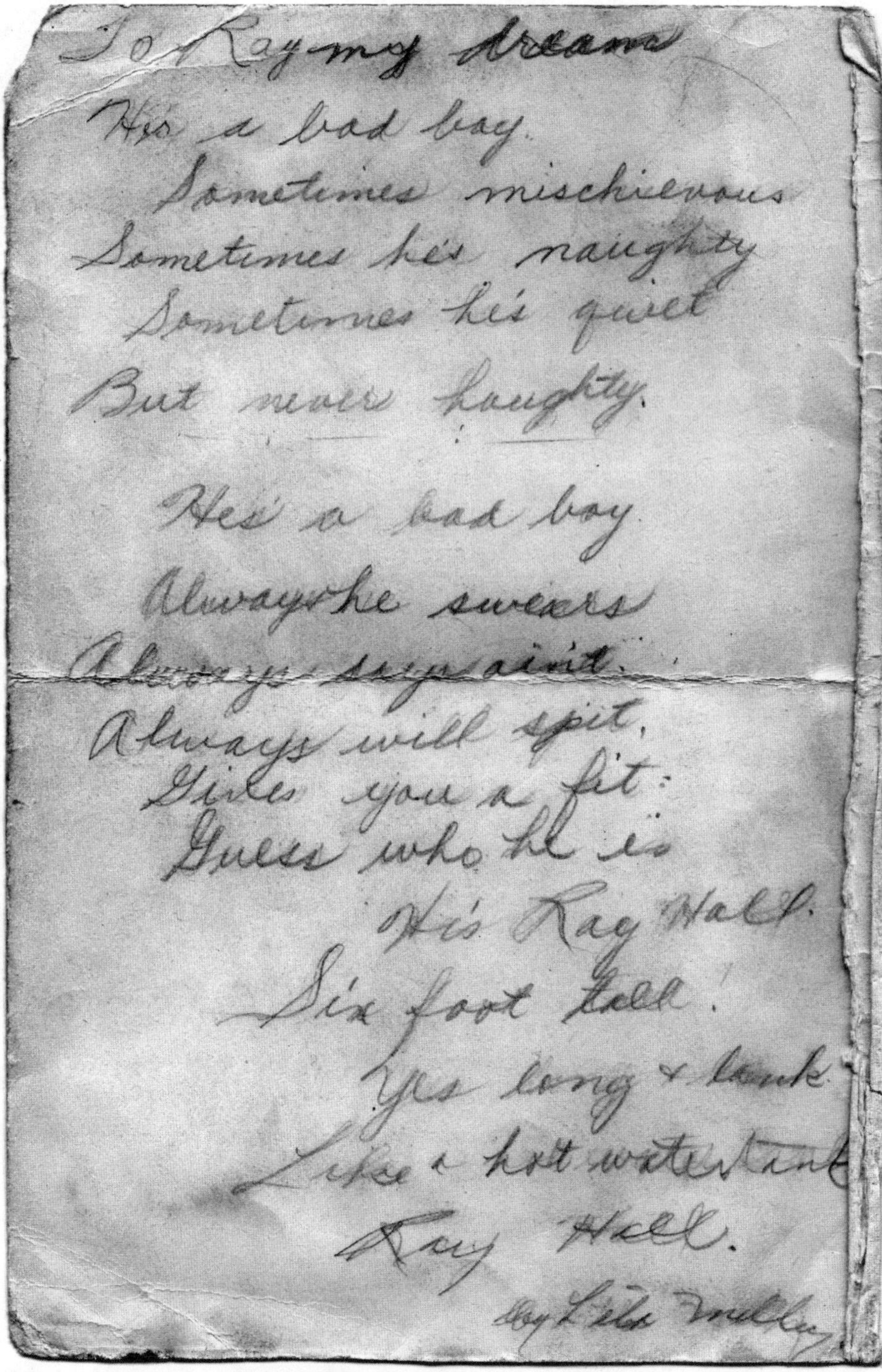

To Ray my dream

He's a bad boy.
Sometimes mischievous
Sometimes he's naughty
Sometimes he's quiet
But never haughty.

He's a bad boy
Always he swears
Always says ain't
Always will spit,
Gives you a fit.
Guess who he is
He's Ray Hall.
Six foot tall.
Yes long & lank
Like a hot water tank
Ray Hall.
By Lila Milley

Lila's grade nine school poem to Ray. Sheep Creek, 1939.

and see who she wants and come back and tell me." I don't know why we did not figure out a plan, like having two whistles for me, three for him, and one for the both of us.

There were four years between Ray and me, so as most boys do with younger sisters, he would try to leave me behind to be by himself or with his pals. He also loved to tease me and call me "Sis," unless he was tattling on me to Mom about something I did, and then he would call me "Shirley." I would get so angry with him that I would flail my arms around, trying to do him some damage. Ray was a tall boy with an easygoing personality; he would react by putting his hand on top of my head, all the while laughing at my useless attempts to reach him. Mom would often stand by watching us and say, "Oh, stop it, you two." Ray grew to be six foot two. One of the girls, Lila Melby, used to describe Ray as being "long and lank as a hot water tank." I think she was sweet on him. Lila wrote a poem to Ray on a small piece of paper, which I have kept all these years.

THE ROAD THAT went through our town followed Sheep Creek. The working mills, the Gold Belt, the Queen, the Motherlode, and the Kootenay Belle, were allowed to dump their tailings into Sheep Creek. The creek, fed by Wulf (Waldie) Lake, Panther Lake, and Curtis Lake, flowed straight by the concentrators into the Salmo River. The tailings left a grey residue that looked like it was dry, but if you stood on it and tapped your feet, it became jelly-like. We children played in the creek all the time, as it was the only place we could keep cool in the hot summer.

Jimmy Younie had a big St. Bernard named Chief that used to lie in the creek to keep cool while we played. He was our gang's dog. He later went blind for some reason; we kids always suspected it was from the stuff in the water. Today, we know that creek was laced with cyanide and arsenic from the tailings, as those were main ingredients in the process of separating the gold from the crushed rock. Exposing the cyanide to sunlight, air, and water was supposed to make the tailings less toxic, so either no one was concerned we could be harmed, or else we never told our parents that we were playing in the tailings and the grey water. Some adult probably told us not to play in the creek where it flowed downstream from the mills, but I have no recollection of it

The only place we had for swimming in the creek was just above the Gold Belt Mill; the water was clean there, but icy cold. On a hot summer day, if we wanted to swim, we would go up to this sort of pool or deep spot in the creek that you could sit in. I remember one July day when we had gone up to the swimming hole and there was still dirty ice on the slide that had come down during the spring melt. When I think of that day, I can still feel that icy water from the snowmelt coming down from a last winter's snow fall. No wonder I never learned to swim until I was an adult, and then only in a heated swimming pool.

ABOUT A YEAR after we had arrived in Sheep Creek, Dad left his job cooking for the Kootenay Belle Mine. The agent he was working for was not getting the supplies and the quality of food he needed to feed the miners. During the Depression, when a lot of men needed jobs, some companies took advantage of this and paid low wages and cut back on the quality of the food. This really bothered Dad, so he quit the job. I had not been haunting the cookhouse the way I did when we first moved there, so I hadn't even known there was a problem until I saw a man at the house from the Queen Mill. The foreman there had heard about Dad quitting and within hours was at our front door, asking Dad to work for him at the mill's concentrator. Dad quickly accepted his offer but asked if he could have a couple of days off first. That was the end of Dad's cooking career; he retired his apron after cooking for the Kootenay Belle. Dad always said cooking was a hard job, anyway. The best thing about him quitting was that he had the weekends off. Now we could go to town on Saturdays!

Working at a concentrator was not something new for Dad—that was what he had been doing in Alamo when he met Mom years before. As I was a curious kid and always full of questions, I asked Dad if I could come and see how the concentrator worked, and he agreed. A concentrator is the treatment plant for the ore to separate the gold from the rock, or waste. My understanding of the process was that the slurry from the ball mill (a kind of grinder) that crushed the ore and rock got stuck on some flat wheels. This slurry was made up of the crushed ore and rock, plus the lime and cyanide added during the grinding process. As the wheels went around, the stuff on the wheels fell off into a huge vat, and somehow through a series of agitators, tanks and filters, the gold mass was separated, leaving behind the waste (or tailings). The gold that was extracted then went through a drying and refining process to remove other impurities before being heated in an oval-shaped furnace until it became molten. The molten gold was then poured into bar molds with the mill's mark and cooled.

Ray at the flume on Sheep Creek, just below our house, 1940. The mines were allowed to dump their tailings into Sheep Creek. The flume channelled fresh water from above the mills for domestic use. The flume also concentrated the flow to a substation to help generate water-powered electricity that the mines and town used until 1934, when most of the power was provided by West Kootenay Power Company.

Ray and Gus standing on the flume on Sheep Creek, 1940.
Note the house in the background with stairs leading down to the creek.

The bars were then sent to the assay office at the post office and kept in a vault until it was time to transport them to the smelter. I was about twelve at the time that I saw the workings of a concentrator, so to any miners reading this, remember I was just a kid and that is how it looked to me.

When I was about thirteen, a girlfriend, Bertha Boyer, and I wanted to go into a mine to see what it was like. Her dad, Leo, was a miner at the Gold Belt Mine. I don't remember if it was her dad who took us, but I do

A Sunday walk with the girls. *L–R*: Hanna, Grace Louise McDonough (standing),
Ruth, Bertha Boyer. I was taking the picture. Sheep Creek, ca. 1941.

vividly remember the trip down into the Gold Belt Mine. We went down in the hoist, a rickety wire cage hung from the top by a heavy cable. We were lowered down about three levels to a tunnel, where there was a very large open area. This was where the men were working. The air temperature was warm to hot underground, and some of the men said they liked the warmth in the wintertime. All the miners wore hard hats with an open-flamed lamp on the front that burned carbide. It was very noisy with the air drills drilling deep holes into the rocks to plant the explosives. Needless to say, my friend and I were more than ready to leave soon after we got there. When we got back to the surface, we both said that we would never work in a place like that! As bad as it was, though, it was still cleaner than a coal mine, except for the silica dust. Silicosis was a lung disease common in the gold miners who worked underground; they inhaled the silica dust, since they never wore masks.

FOREST FIRES WERE a common occurrence in our heavily forested valley home. One summer, when I was ten and Ray was fourteen, a forest fire started just across the road from our house. Dad, Mom, and our neighbours were standing in front of our homes watching the men fighting the fire when Ray decided he wanted to help, frightening us all by running toward the fire. Dad yelled, "Get back here!" If Ray wasn't chasing bears, he was chasing forest fires.

A little earlier that day, Dad had given me a ten-cent piece, and I now held it in my hand. Watching the fire, I began to worry, so I pushed the dime back into Dad's hand. He asked me what I was doing. I said, "We might need this." He laughed and said, "No, it will be all right." The men were able to put out the fire quickly before it spread. Dad was always good about giving us coins. He gave them to his grandchildren, too, in the years to come. At that time, five cents would buy you a big chocolate bar.

One summer, the Catholic church put on a summer school for the children, to keep them from boredom, no doubt. One of my friends and I decided to attend without informing our parents. It was fun; we coloured a lot, which is still one of my favourite pastimes. My mother could not find me anywhere, and she had a tendency to panic when that happened. When I came home for supper, she asked me where I had been. I was honest and told her. She was aghast at and exclaimed, "Oh! Your grandfather would roll over in his grave if he knew that!"

You see, Grandfather Phylander Johnson was an Orangeman, a man of Protestant faith, as was Great-Grandfather John Dillon, Grandmother Eliza Johnson's father. In the 1800s Great-Grandfather John Dillon's mother sent him to New York City from Ireland when he was still a boy, after both his father and elder brother were killed by Catholic men with nationalist party views. This would mean that Great-Great-Grandfather Dillon was also an Orangeman, and a Protestant, with unionism views. Great-Grandfather Dillon's mother said they were not going to get her other son, too, so she sent John to New York. This is what Mom meant about my grandfather rolling over in his grave. Needless to say, I did not go back to the Catholic summer school, but I still did not understand why.

Every time I hear or sing the hymn, "Onward Christian Soldiers," I think of an incident that happened one Sunday in Sheep Creek. My friend Grace McDonough and I were walking on the road near the store, by the bridge across from the school, when we met this little coupé. It belonged to Reverend Mott, the United Church minister from Trail. He came up to Sheep Creek once a month to hold a church service in the school. Mr. Mott stopped and asked Grace and me if we would come to the service with him. As young children, we were all taught never to take candy or rides from strange men. I asked my mother why, but I don't remember what she said, except, "Don't do it!" I am sure Grace and I trusted Reverend Mott, because we did know him, and he was a fine man. So we discussed it a bit, and told him if he would let us sing "Onward Christian Soldiers," we would come. He agreed, and we met him at the school. There was only one other person at the service, one of the men from the mines. I have never forgotten how this good minister came all the way from Trail to hold a church service for one person and two ten-year-old children. And, yes, we did sing "Onward Christian Soldiers."

As we got older, my girlfriends and I usually took a Sunday walk down Sheep Creek Road toward Salmo. Sometimes we would bring a camera and take pictures. I have a picture from one Sunday afternoon of us girls sitting on a bridge that crossed over Sheep Creek. I remember the water flowing in the creek would be a solid grey with the tailings from the mills.

I WAS TWELVE years old when Mom was sent word that Grandma Johnson, her mother, was ill and not expected to live. In those days, the CPR was the main way to travel. The line from Vancouver that stopped in Nelson headed east at 1:30 a.m. It was late February of 1939 when the letter

Aunt Grace and me going for a ride with Tiny, the Shetland pony that took us to school, while Mom and I were visiting Aunt Edna in Greenway, Manitoba, 1939.

came, and my parents decided that Mom and I should go. It meant that I would be out of school and that Ray would stay home with Dad. Mom and I packed our suitcases, headed the thirty miles to the Nelson train station, and got on board. Then Mom decided not to go, so back home to Sheep Creek we went.

Two weeks later, another letter came saying that if Mom wanted to see her mother alive one more time, she had better come right away. The decision was made, and we were on our way to Greenway, Manitoba, to visit family I had only heard about. I don't remember much about the long ride across Alberta and Saskatchewan to Winnipeg, but I remember the experience of sleeping in the sleeper car on the train.

Mom's brother, Roy, picked us up in Winnipeg and drove us to Greenway, where I had my first visit and last glimpse of my grandmother, Maggie Eliza Dillon Johnson. Mom stayed in town with Uncle Bert, and Uncle Bill brought Aunt Edna, Mom's sister, into town to stay with them. Uncle Bill took me back to the farm to be with my cousins. It was a March evening, lit by the moon, for our cold ride to the farm in a horse-drawn sleigh. I stayed warm, all wrapped up in a real buffalo robe. I found it all very exciting.

I had a great time on the farm. I finally met all my cousins. Because school was still in, I was introduced to Tiny, a Shetland pony, who pulled us all to school in a cart. The school my cousins, Opal, Iris, and Keith, attended was out on the prairie. The older cousins, Joyce, and Lex, who was so very handsome, had outgrown school.

The school had three-seater seats. I had seen this kind of seating in pictures, but this was the real thing. To this day, every time I see a photo of a lone school and an outhouse in the middle of the prairie, I think of that school. I learned how to sing, "Little Sir Echo" while I attended, but I don't remember anything else. Just being there with my cousins was an experience!

There were sheep on the farm. One day while coming home from school, the kids spotted a wee, newborn lamb that had been abandoned by its mother. My cousins gave the lamb to me, and I put it inside my coat. We took it to the farm, where I helped care for it and fed it milk from a bottle. The shed where the lambs were kept had an open window space, and my cousin Keith put a small plank against it to create a doorway. We would watch the lambs run in a circle, up and down the plank and through this window, bleating as they ran. They sure had fun.

Another memory was of a big stallion that belonged to a neighbour. I think the rider was a friend of cousin Lex. I had no idea a horse could be so strong, wild and nearly uncontrollable. The fellow riding it must have known what he was doing, because that horse reared up on his hind legs and pawed the air just like in the movies. I was in awe of the stallion's powerful and beautiful spirit.

We stayed a month at the farm, until Grandma Johnson passed away at the end of April. When I came home, I was, "as brown as a berry," from the prairie sun and wind. Everyone said I looked so good, as I also had gained some weight; I had always been a skinny girl.

MOM HAD A good sense of humour. A good example of this was when Mary, a neighbour and friend who lived just down the road from us, was visiting one day. Mom and Mary and I got into a friendly argument about something. Mom loved to argue her point of view, but this time she could see that she was losing, so she got up out of her chair, walked into the bedroom, and closed the door. While Mary and I wondered what she was up to, we continued our conversation, not thinking much more about what had just happened. Well, in a few minutes the bedroom door opened, and there was Mom, her best hat sitting askew on her head, wearing her coat (which was misbuttoned), with a suitcase in one hand and a dry chamber pot hanging from other. She looked over our heads, seemingly filled with indignation, and said very firmly, "All right! If that's the way you feel, I'm leaving home!" As Mary and I just sat there with our mouths hanging open, she headed for the door. Then we all collapsed with laughter. Needless to say, that was the end of the argument.

In the summer of 1939, I was twelve. Grandma and Grandpa Hall had just moved from the Fairview district of Nelson to Vancouver, taking cousin Ruth with them. I had wanted to come to Nelson that summer for a holiday and be near the beautiful Lakeside Park beach just down from Grandma Hall's, but now that my grandparents and cousin were gone, there was no one left to hang out with and no place to stay in Nelson. I talked to Bertha Boyer about this, and we decided to ask our moms if we could go together and stay in Nelson for a few days. Mom had a good friend in Fairview and asked her if we two girls could board with her for a few days. Mom's friend agreed, and we both happily settled into our room when we got to Nelson. We went to the beach every day, played in the water, read, and, of course, talked about cute boys. We had a very nice time on our mini-holiday, enough to ask our moms if we could go again the following summer. We never did go, though, as the whole world was about to change, including ours.

When the world began to talk about war in the fall of 1939, we kids all talked about it, too. We were very excited at the prospect, having absolutely no concept of what it was all about; it just sounded so exciting. It was difficult not to feel patriotic with all the recruitment posters around. Our teacher, Mr. Unsworth, tried to tell us that it would not be fun at all. We thought he was a coward, because he said he would not join the army, seeing as he was at the age that was wanted for soldiers. I wonder if he ever did fight in the war.

The author, almost fifteen years old, February 20, 1942, in Sheep Creek. PHOTO BY MYERS STUDIOS.

NELSON: BEGINNINGS TO ENDINGS

Mom was a forward-looking lady. She was thirty and still single when she met Dad. She had received a business education and had worked for the *Winnipeg Free Press* prior to her marriage. Mom always wanted me to have a higher education. In those days, if you were a woman who wanted to work outside the home, your options were to become a nurse, a teacher, or an office worker. Despite this, I had my sights firmly set on becoming a portrait painter. There was a portrait painter named Philip Alexius De László in Spain who captured my attention, but for the time being, Mom wished for me to finish high school. She wanted very badly for me to be able to support myself in case the need arose. Mom also felt that every wife should have a bank account of her own. That was pretty modern thinking for a lady born in the late 1800s. I never really thought about how she felt about Ray and his future. I think she left that to Dad. Ray had no inclinations to become a cook. I don't even remember him boiling water!

In September 1941, when I was fourteen, Mom and Dad arranged for me to go to Nelson to start grade ten at Nelson High School. Some of our friends had moved to town already, including Mrs. Lindsley, a friend from Beaton and Camborne. She agreed to give me room and board and watch over me during the week, since she was living alone at that time. I would take the Greyhound bus home Friday night to Salmo, and Dad would drive down to pick me up so I could spend the weekends at home.

I was still boarding at Mrs. Lindsley's when Bertha Boyer's family moved from Sheep Creek to the Fairview district in Nelson. Bertha and I asked our parents if it would be okay if I stayed with them, so I ended

I took the Greyhound bus Friday night to Salmo, where Dad picked me up to spend the weekend at home. The Christian Science Church on Baker Street is in the background. TOUCHSTONES NELSON MUSEUM OF ART AND HISTORY, TNNDN091

Ray at home for New Year's, proudly wearing an army uniform. Sheep Creek, 1943.

up boarding with the Boyer family in Fairview, just a few blocks from Grandma and Grandpa Hall's former home, the one Dad and Uncle Hugh had built. It was a pleasant time. Bertha and I were starting to experiment with makeup and argued over who had the longest eyelashes. She won.

This was also kind of a sad time for us because our town, Sheep Creek, was being deserted. I think most of the residents moved to Nelson. The single men from the bunkhouses either went away to join the armed forces or else found work in other mines, especially the ones needed for the war effort. Dad was still working at the Queen Mill, so Mom and Dad stayed behind in Sheep Creek.

Ray was now eighteen. After he finished grade nine in Sheep Creek, he was not interested in continuing on to high school, so when it came time for him to find himself a place in the world, he asked to go to the Clough Ranch. He had been working at the ranch for two years by this time and liked the farm work, the cows, and the life there. Going into the mine did not appeal to him, but now that he was of legal age, he applied for clearance papers to work in the mines anyway. After my short visit to a mine, I certainly did not want that kind of work for him either. In November 1942, Ray was home when he received his clearance from the mining company. He was considering whether to go to work in the mines or join the navy, as Jimmy Younie had done, but as luck would have it, he was called up for military service instead. I'm not sure how Ray felt about getting his call-to-active-duty letter, but I think he felt patriotic and excited over the prospects of adventure in another country. Mom and Dad had already gone through this experience once together in the First World War, so I think they were sad and afraid for Ray, but they hid it well and gave him a great deal of strength and support. I admired his courage, of course, and I was going to miss him, but I was also excited that he was going on a new adventure. My feelings about this would change drastically in years to come. Ray left for Vancouver before Christmas to report for his post. By January 1943, he had been inducted into the army. He came home for a few days at New Year's, proudly wearing an army uniform. We spent one of those days, just the two of us, hanging out together in Nelson, where he took me to see the film *Holiday Inn*.

When Ray was drafted into the army in 1941, just after he turned eighteen, he had to fill out a form about his vital statistics. I helped him with his measurements. He had to measure his chest, so I did it and gave him the result. He didn't look very happy with the number I gave him. Then he said to do it again, but this time he took in a deep breath first. When I told him the second measurement, with his chest expanded, he remarked, with wonder and a sad expression, "Gee, it's the same as before." I felt sorry for him, but pretty soon we started to giggle.

On December 7, 1941, I was at home in Sheep Creek. I was almost fifteen. There were six inches of fresh snow on the ground that Sunday morning. I was walking down the road toward the house at about ten in the morning when I heard someone call out that the Japanese had bombed Pearl Harbor. I stood stunned; all the sounds in the forest that were muffled from the new-fallen snow were now drowned out by my heartbeat as I ran back home to tell Mom and Dad the news. It was a shock to everyone. The United States declared war against Japan the next day.

Canada was already at war. Little did I think that Ray would lose his life in Italy within three years, so very far from home. So would his friend Hank Birkland, a flight lieutenant in the Royal Canadian Air force, who also flew Spitfires for the Royal Air Force Fighter Command. Hank was captured by the enemy after his plane was shot down. He was a key member of the famous "Great Escape" tunnelling operation from the prisoner-of-war camp Stalag Luft III in Poland. He was recaptured three days after his escape and faced a firing squad on March 31, 1944. Hank had come to Sheep Creek, like many other single men looking for mining work, during the Depression. He was a gold miner at the Gold Belt Mine and lived at the bunkhouse when we lived there. Ray liked Hank. Hank was a few years older than Ray and had qualities that I think Ray admired.

The war also brought an end to our town. The owners of Kootenay Belle Gold Mines partnered with Whitewater Mines, who owned a group of zinc, ore, and galena mines at Whitewater, near Bear and Fish Lakes, between Kaslo and New Denver. I was told they moved all the mining and concentrator equipment to those mines in 1943. The Canadian government was not as interested in gold anymore, as there was a new high demand for lead and other base metals for the war effort.

In May 1943, with the mines closing in Sheep Creek and Ray and me gone from home, Mom and Dad decided to move to Nelson. I was glad to be living with them again, but felt a little sad; once again, the mines forced us to pull up roots and find a new home. Dad put the house in Sheep Creek up for sale. He ended up selling the house for the worth of its lumber. Our good friend Paul Lieb from Camborne bought it and reused the lumber to build Ida and himself a new house near the Yankee Girl Mill in Ymir. You can see the house from the highway. I still notice it every time we drive in that direction; it does bring back memories. I don't know who ended up finding my little greyhound racetrack in the attic, but I imagined it bringing joy to some new child.

We moved into an apartment at the old Strathcona Hotel on the corner of Victoria and Stanley Streets in Nelson while Mom and Dad scouted for a house to buy. Four blocks up the hill from the Strathcona Hotel, close

Strathcona Hotel at 606 Stanley Street, Nelson, ca. 1925. We lived there
for a few months while Mom and Dad looked for a house to purchase.
TOUCHSTONES NELSON MUSEUM OF ART AND HISTORY, TN-83.169.29

to the corner of Stanley and Latimer, Mom and Dad were happy to find a
two-bedroom house for sale at 313 Latimer Street, next to the Anglican
Manse. They rented it for a while, then finally bought it from a widowed
lady. Latimer Street is historically important for being named in the 1891
survey by Frank Herbert Latimer. Our old house still stands there today.
It was a perfect location. Nelson High School was only four blocks up
Latimer at the corner of Hendryx Street, and it was close to Dad's future
job, so we were both able to come home on our lunch hours. The streetcar barns, where Dad would eventually get a new job as a conductor and

Our house on Latimer Street: Author leaning on the fence that Dad built in 1943.
Mom's flower garden, ca. 1950. Dad must have got tired of fixing and painting
the fence and replaced it with a not so pretty new one. Also gone is the
large chestnut from in front of the house, ca. 1960, Nelson.

motorman on the Electric Street Car Service, were located just up around
the corner from our house.

The money used to pay off the house was what we received from the
Canadian government after Ray was killed. I wonder how many people
realize that every soldier, airman, and sailor had made out a will and that
the government had a duty to carry it out. The payment didn't typically
amount to a lot of money but in our case, it was enough for the remain-
ing money owed on the house. I always felt it was a suitable thing to
do with the funds; Ray gave the last of himself to his family's need and
in some way was still a part of our home, even if he was not to able to
return to it.

Our home on Latimer Street was different than the other places we
had lived in, because this time we owned the land, too. We also had paved
streets lined on either side with beautiful mature horse-chestnut trees.
Our city lot had a lean-to at the back, which served as Dad's garage until
he built another one. The front yard was only as wide as the house, but
Dad fenced in this miniature yard with a white scrolled lattice metal

fence on a wood frame so Mom could plant a flower garden. I finally discovered garden flowers, which look quite different from wild mountain flowers. Our new house also had indoor plumbing and a big bathtub for Mom, although it still did not sit in a field of flowers. The fence came in handy, too, for a couple of boys to lean on while we discussed our futures after dark.

The heating in our new home was somewhat strange to me, as we had only ever had a woodstove and oil lamps for that purpose. Now we had two gas heaters, which burned with a hissing blue flame and were fed by a gas line maintained by the Nelson Coke and Gas Works Corporation. We had a gas stove as well as a woodstove in our kitchen for cooking. The gas heaters always made me feel a little uncomfortable; I was glad when Dad dug out the basement to put in a furnace. A few years later, he had insulation blown into the ceiling, which helped keep the house warmer. The house had high ceilings, so all the heat would rise and get wasted. Houses built back then were not typically insulated. The interior walls of our new home were finished with lath and plaster, and painted a pretty off-white, unlike the unfinished, rough-wood stud walls of our previous homes. Mind you, I had never disliked our other houses in the mountains; they could be quite cozy. It was really nice to finally have a furnished home, as we had never had much furniture while living in the mining towns—although, of course, the Clough Ranch had furniture, as did Grandma and Grandpa Hall's place in Nelson. I wonder whatever became of our old Winnipeg couch that Ray used to sleep on.

DAD WAS AN early riser, and he had a habit of opening the front door wide for ten minutes or so, when he got up, year round. It happened that my bedroom door was next to it. I would call out, "Close the door!" even though I was under a quilt or two. Dad's answer would always be, "It is easier to warm fresh air than stale." I would grumble and crawl even deeper under my quilt. He would tease, "You must be tired holding up all those covers."

Those quilts I am talking about were Mom's homemade quilts, which we had in Sheep Creek. They were made with sheep's wool that came from our Manitoba relatives' farm. They were like the duvets of today, but with no feathers. Mom tied her quilts together with yarn instead of sewing through them because of their thickness, which also made the quilts quite fluffy. I remember helping her with this finishing touch on each new quilt.

Streetcar No. 23 and motormen in uniform of the Nelson Street Railway, Lakeside Park, 1940s.
L–R: Les Hall, Alf Manson, Dave Webster, Scotty McCandlish, Alex Dingwall, Lee Hall,
Lou Blakey, Roy Canfield, Bill Cartwright, Bill Leslie, Jack Robinson, Charlie Bunce. Today,
the streetcar is fully restored and runs through Lakeside Park in the summer months.
DAVE WEBSTER COLLECTION, NELSON ELECTRIC TRAMWAY SOCIETY

The cover itself was usually made of scraps from her other sewing projects. The most popular design at the time was the log-cabin motif, but women were inventing new designs then as now. Mom made these quilts and most of our clothes using her Singer sewing machine. These machines were in nice wood cabinets in those days; the folding lids provided more room for the material.

Before living in Nelson, we had never had a house phone. The only telephone in a home I knew of was the one at the ranch in Slocan, and it

The original streetcar barn was on Hall Mines Road, about half a block up the hill and around the corner from our house on Latimer Street.

NELSON ELECTRIC TRAMWAY SOCIETY

was for Uncle Wat's work with the CPR and not for the kids. In fact, I don't know of any family having a telephone in their home in the mining camps. But we were in the city now, and most people did have a telephone, but still not us, for a long time. There was a telephone shortage, during the war years, because the telephone manufacturers were repurposed to support the war effort. The closest telephone to our house was at the streetcar barn where Dad took a job; however, that was for company use only. Sometimes though, when Dad was at work, I would go to the streetcar barn, and if it was just him there, I would ask really nicely, and he would let me sneak in a quick phone call to a friend to meet me somewhere. Or I would walk to a friend's place when I wanted to visit or make plans with them. I was about seventeen when we finally got a phone.

When Mom and Dad moved to Nelson, for the first time in his life, it was difficult for Dad to find work. Dad was now over fifty and living in a city instead of a mining town. He was close to retirement age, so starting a new career was difficult and he had no desire to go back to being a cook. It was Dad's friend, Mr. Norman Stibbs, the mayor of Nelson, who put in a good word for him at some of the local businesses.

Dad first got a job maintaining the furnaces for the City of Nelson Gaol, the city lockup, at the corner of 606 Victoria Street. In a short time, he became a night guard, keeping watch mostly over the local disorderly drunk, who was regularly put in the drunken tank for the night until he sobered up. Dad said that such men were harmless and he claimed he often didn't even lock the cell door. He also worked temporarily for the city at the Nelson landfill, when the trash was dumped on the land between Kootenay Lake and the CPR line. During the war, rubber, glass, metal, paper, animal fat, and clothing were some of the items recycled to use in the war effort. It was important to monitor what was thrown into the landfill as trash and what was put on the trains to be taken to other places, where the materials could be recycled and reused. Today, the landfill is the site of Nelson's airfield, which was built in 1947 and dedicated to Norman Stibbs, Dad's friend and the former mayor of Nelson.

It wasn't long before Dad was offered another city job, this time with the Nelson Street Railway Company—first as a conductor collecting the fares and taking care of the passengers, and then later as a motorman (operating the streetcar) on Streetcar No. 23. It was an easy walk for Dad to get to work: the streetcar barn was on Hall Mines Road, about half a block up the hill and around the corner from our house. What more could you ask for! Dad worked as a motorman on Streetcar No. 23 until 1949, when city buses replaced streetcars and he retired. He and Mom spent the rest of their lives living contentedly in Nelson and visiting relatives on the Clough Ranch.

Other than walking or riding a bike, the streetcar was the only other way for us kids to get around in Nelson at that time. However, it didn't come without its hazards on the steep streets of Nelson. The many bigleaf maple trees dropped leaves onto the tracks, and in the wet weather, the leaves would stick together and start to decay and create a very slippery condition known as "black rails." This was very dangerous on the parts of Nelson's streets where the streetcar had a steep street to climb or descend. I remember riding the street car under this condition; it was like riding greased lightning, as there was very little friction for the streetcar brakes to slow us down. Then there were the mischievous boys who would throw leaves on the tracks just for fun. I remember when one runaway streetcar went straight down Stanley, crossed over Baker Street, left the tracks, and went down the hill to end up in Hoods Bakery on the highway. To help fix this situation, the city used special streetcar sweepers to clean the rails of leaves and debris and of snow and ice in the winter.

I WAS GROWING up fast, becoming more self-conscious about my clothes and more interested in fashion. Mom had made me a new wardrobe of clothes for high school; I was a little embarrassed to tell the city girls that my mother had made all my clothes. I was afraid they would think I was from a poor, small mining town and unsophisticated. It was after June Cuthbert, one of my new high school friends, said, "Shirley, don't feel bad, these are custom, handmade clothes, just for you," that I quickly got over feeling embarrassed. In fact, later, when I needed a new coat, I found a picture of a lovely one in the catalogue and showed it to Mom. I designed the coat, Aunt Grace made a pattern for it, and Mom sewed it. It was a lovely royal-blue colour, with a cape sewn into the coat; this was very fashionable during wartime. Some years later, I twigged to what pattern books were all about. My conclusion was that the people who sewed their own clothes were the ones who decided the next new styles. The pattern companies simply watched to see what patterns sold, and then the manufacturers went to work. I think I came to this conclusion because every time I chose to make a new garment, be it a coat or dress or whatever, I seemed to be the only one wearing that style, and by the time I wore it out, or tired of it, suddenly it became the style every other woman was wearing! Would you agree with my conclusion?

In Sheep Creek, I had finished grade nine, which was when the older kids, including me, were considered the most "grown up," but in Nelson, there were many more students my age and, in my eyes, more mature. How was I going to fit in? I knew my manners and how to be polite to others, but how to act more mature than a "hillbilly" kid?! The first one to take me under her wing was June Cuthbert. June had nice clothes, and she was kind to me. Our friendship was outside of school. She was a little

Trying to hitch a ride from Lee Hall's streetcar in front of the house on Latimer Street
in Nelson: Edith Williams, the author, and Fay House, ca. 1944. The neighbour's
car barn across the street in the background is still there today.

older than me, so we were not in the same grade or classes. She lived with
her family in an apartment above one of the businesses on Baker Street.
Her father owned a car dealership, also near Baker Street, where he sold
new cars.

When June told me I was lucky to have my clothes especially made just
for me, instead of purchased off a store clothes rack, she won my friendship. I was, of course, still very self-conscious at school. I tried to act
confident, but not overconfident. I tried to be sophisticated, but was not
mature enough and only embarrassed myself. I never realized at that time
that there were others who felt the same way too.

In Nelson, everybody felt like a stranger to me, except maybe June. In
the mining towns, everyone had known everyone else in our two-room
school, but in Nelson there were so many classes of grade ten that I didn't
know anyone. Once I moved back home with Mom and Dad, I hardly saw
Bertha Boyer, as she had chosen the business classes, which were separate
from general high school classes.

I found this kind of sad, because Bertha and I had grown quite close to
each other. I remember that she even shared with me how her family had
been victims of the revolution in Russia and how they had fled for their

Annie Karchie and the author
showing off the ribbons they won
at the Salmo Races, July 1, 1939.

lives when the Communist Party took over. Bertha said that they packed their money and clothes and fled for another country. She described how along the way, they had stopped at an empty house to rest, but because the Bolshevik police were close behind, they hid their money in the chimney of the house. When the police had caught up with them the first thing they did was to light the fire in the stove because it was cold outside, burning up all the money they hid. She said they managed to get away and make it to Canada, but poor and with very few possessions. Maybe Bertha had a better sense as to what was about to come with the war than the rest of us kids.

Despite my new fashion sense, I was still every little bit of the tomboy I had been back in Sheep Creek. At about age eleven, I had started competing in the annual summer sports days held in May in Ymir, behind the big hall in a field that was always full of yellow buttercups, and the ones held in Salmo on July 1, at a sports field in the park. I would enter the event competitions for broad jump, high jump, and several of the sprint races. I loved stepping into the running blocks. I would get so excited that I would get "jimmy legs," and then when the starting pistol went off, I would be off, quick as a bunny. I don't ever remember practising for any of the events,

Nelson High School sports day at the Civic Centre field, ca. 1943.
The author is at the high jump. The scissor kick was the most
common technique used in high jumping at that time.

or if I did, it was very little. I do remember, however, that I could hardly walk for a week after all of the events. I always placed among the top three winners, usually taking first prize in the sprint event. The prizes were cash in fifty- and twenty-five cent pieces, which was a lot of money for a kid in those days. I would make all my summer spending money at the sports events. My favourite sport was track. When I went into high school, I continued to compete in the same events during Nelson's high school sports day at the Civic Centre field. There was no room for these activities around the high school on Latimer Street, because the playing field was small, sloping, and usually swampy.

Nelson High had a curling team that would practise and compete on the curling sheets at the Civic Centre. I was in grade twelve when the sport of "jam can" curling reached schools across the west. Curling had become an adult competitive club sport in the Kootenay region in the late 1800s. A typical curling rock was made from special granite quarried in Europe, then shaped to a standard size and weight. The curling rocks were heavy and expensive, too expensive for a kid to own; thus came the invention of jam can curling.

Nelson High School girls' curling team, 1943. *L–R*: Dodi Ward, the author, Bev McCosham, and Carol Perdu. The Civic Centre, at 719 Vernon Street in Nelson, has the oldest operating arena and skating rink in British Columbia, and a sports museum.

The idea of making curling rocks from jam cans first originated with the Prairie people, but it caught on quickly in the "Queen City," Nelson. The four-pound jam cans we used to make our rocks came from the local jam factory. Our moms would buy the large cans of jam that we used for our jam can curling rocks from the MacDonald Jam Factory. The building, at 303 Vernon Street was designed by local architect Alexander Carrie and built in 1911 by James Albert McDonald. Our parents saved the empty jam cans, then we would smooth out the bottom edges of the can with a hammer to make it slide more easily on the ice; then we would fill them with cement, fashion a metal handle, and wait for the cement to cure. I presume the curling club shuddered every time one of us threw our so-called rock down the ice.

I was the skip of our school's girls' curling team. Bev McCosham, Dodi Ward, and Carol Perdu were my teammates. I would get very excited once I threw the rock, and I would yell "Sweep! Sweep!" at the sweepers. My excitement did not always go over so well, especially with the ladylike girls. Bev, who thought I was a little overly aggressive in my enthusiasm and not very ladylike, was sure to tell me, albeit in a gentle tone, "Shirley, I don't like it when you yell at me."

Nelson Civic Centre and fields, with Royal Canadian Air Cadets training in 1941,
pipe players wearing the tartan kilt in background. Nelson families hosted them.

Each person was issued a ration book and food stamps by the Canadian government,
which allowed them to buy food and supplies that were in short supply in wartime.

Our high school had lots of extracurricular activities, including football, basketball, hockey, as well as band music, though track meets were my favourite. One time, a high school band came on an exchange to our high school from Coeur d'Alene, Idaho. They needed billets for the musicians. One of the girls was Japanese. Canada and its allies were at war with Japan at the time, so Mr. Rogers, our principal, was sensitive as to which family that girl might feel the most comfortable staying with. He asked me if I would billet the girl while the band was visiting. I felt very honoured that he asked me. Our Slocan family was friendly with the Japanese-Canadian internees up the valley and bore them no ill, nor did we. Jane was a nice girl; we wrote to one another for a while after she returned home.

Nelson's Civic Centre and its sports field on Vernon Street were fairly new; they were built in 1935. It was an important gathering place for school events and non-school activities—a place where kids could watch live theatre and movies or play basketball and other sports in the gymnasium all year round, including figure skating, ice hockey, and curling in winter. Its outdoor track and field and baseball diamonds got plenty of use during the warmer seasons. During the war, the sports field also served as training grounds for cadets.

WHEN I THINK back on wartime, Jim Hoover is a name I can never forget. He was noted as the first student who joined up and was then killed in action in what seemed to be a very short period of time. His story certainly brought this European war close to our school and us kids. Sylvia Crook's book *Homefront and Battlefront: Nelson BC in World War II*, published in 2005, includes a good brief account of who Jim was, just as it does of my brother, Ray, and so many more servicemen.

After the war erupted on September 1, 1939, it became a daily part of life for the next six years and affected many of us, in ways we could never have imagined, for the rest of our lives. We went through food and gas shortages. We walked a lot. Every man, woman, and child had a ration booklet that allowed us to purchase meat, bread, dairy products, and sugar. Buying fresh meat was difficult. We had canned bacon imported from Argentina. The cans were full of grease with a few bits of bacon. All the good stuff went to Europe, I presume to "our Canadian boys." I think there were even ration books for babies. I was not the shopper or the cook in my family; it was left up to Mom to handle all that. Most people tried to grow their own vegetables, planting "Victory Gardens" to help with the food shortage. We also had "meatless" days at restaurants and at home as the war continued and the government reduced the meat rations even further. Our family loved rice pudding, and the only source of rice was in the Slocan Valley, where the Japanese were interned and grew rice that we were able to buy.

There was not much joyriding to speak of during this time. A small group of us classmates would hang together—Fay House, Jack Bone, Alex Freeman, Dave Pearce, and me. On Saturday afternoons, Fay and I would get gussied up and head downtown to go window-shopping at the ladies' wear stores. The clerks would even watch for our visits, but we seldom bought anything—maybe some gloves or some other item once in a while, but we sure learned a lot about dress styles. Mom was still sewing my clothes, so I spent more time in the pattern-book department, where I learned a lot about fashion.

Sundays, when I got together with my pals, we'd go for walks, ride our bikes, or fool around downtown. Not many guys had access to a car, and gasoline was rationed during the war, so this curtailed a lot of other activities young people like to do. Walking or bicycling was the norm for transportation; luckily our house was only five blocks up from the downtown Baker Street shops. Sometimes we would walk up to Rosemont (where there were small farms at that time, not a golf course)—anything at all to escape the constant reminders that there was a war going on.

The movie theatres were always showing war pictures of Europe in the newsreels, and later of Japan, too. The movies themselves were pretty well all war stories, if not of our generation then from another time. Even that cute Civic Theatre doorman, who had worked his way up to assistant manager, had taken off with the army to England. In my last year of high school, I became an usherette, although he did not know it; he was a distant memory, at least for now.

SOUTH NELSON ELEMENTARY School stands today on the site where Nelson High School was located from 1902 to 1956, when the high school moved to a new building on the former Balding Ranch in Fairview. The new Nelson High School was named the L.V. Rogers Secondary School, after our beloved principal, who served Nelson High for twenty-four years, from 1922 to 1946. Principal Rogers had such an impact on student's lives; I recall reading, many years later, in a letter written by my former

A typical Sunday afternoon spent hanging around downtown on Baker Street in Nelson with my pals. *L–R*: Dave Pearce, me (Shirley), Alex Freeman, Fay House, and Jack Bone standing in front of the Royal Bank of Canada, at the corner of Stanley and Baker Streets, ca. 1944

classmate Doug Abby: "The hair-pulling incident reminds me of what simple school kids we were really, and really kids! I will always be grateful for L.V. Rogers and his kind, wise, patient guidance."

The hair-pulling incident that Doug was referring to had taken place one day in Principal Rogers's Latin class, when he was reading to us from our textbook and we were quietly listening. Doug Abby was in the seat behind me. I had put my hair in braids that day. I was engrossed in Mr. Rogers's reading when I felt a sharp tug on one of my braids. This was not the first time I had felt my hair pulled when Doug was behind

Mr. Rogers teaching Latin class, ca. 1944, at Nelson High School.

me; I became so angry at the interruption that I swung my arm straight out behind me. It collided with the side of Doug's head, almost knocking him out of his seat. Dead silence! I looked at Mr. Rogers's face and saw shock, then disappointment at my unladylike behaviour. I quickly said something like, "He was pulling my hair!" There was total silence from the rest of the class. I don't remember what Mr. Rogers said, but the look on his face was enough for me; nothing more needed to be said. I felt awful! I don't remember what happened after that, except that it went no further. In hindsight, I wish I had ignored Doug, as the hair-pulling could never have hurt me as much as my angry reaction and the disappointment of Principal Rogers did. Doug and I worked it out and remained friends. He became a missionary doctor in Botswana. We corresponded for a while, and I saw him with his family on one of their visits home, many years later, in 1980. The episode has stayed with me all my life.

When I was in high school, the term "teenager" was unknown to us; we were known as "young people." Being young meant that you were in the developing stage of growing into adulthood with a future, and not compartmentalized as teens, who were seen as rebellious and still in search of themselves. I won't tell all, just that our victories and defeats were really much more like those of young people today, despite the Depression and the war. Maybe you have different tools to use in solving your particular problems, but handling each situation, setback, or misadventure leads to a solution, sometimes hurtful but always instructive. It is called "growing up."

While we basically had the same temptations and troubles that kids and teens have today, I think we had a lot less peer pressure. The worst temptation we had to deal with was alcohol and many of us, especially the girls, just said, "No!" On Saturday nights in the summer, the older boys and girls would hang out at beach bonfires down at Lakeside and experiment with drinking. Those were the taste-testing times. I tried beer at a couple of beach parties but I thought it was the foulest-tasting drink, so I never drank it again. No one pressured me, or if they did I must have ignored it. When I was eighteen, I tried a sip of whiskey and thought that was horrible-tasting too, so I dumped it out onto the ground, much to my date's horror! I never tried alcohol again after that as I did not find the taste of liquor appealing and I did not get any pleasure from drinking it.

Smoking was a little different for me, even though I was just puffing and not inhaling. A lot of adults smoked during that time so it was more socially accepted. The movies and advertisements were a big influence because they portrayed smoking as sophisticated and cool. I remember the first time I tried a cigarette on a dare, I was sixteen. A group of us young people had been at Wait's News (a coffee, ice cream, and news bar on Baker Street) having a milkshake, and someone dared me to take a few puffs of a cigarette. I thought I would be cool and look glamorous so I decided to give it a try. A few minutes later, someone from the group told me that I didn't look so well. I didn't feel so good either. I went outside for some fresh air in front of Wait's and sat on the curb with my head hung between my knees, then I promptly threw up my milkshake into the gutter. To say the least, I didn't look or feel so glamorous anymore. I didn't try smoking again until a few years later, when my husband would have me roll and light his cigarettes for him while he was driving. One day I realized that I was starting to like the taste of them and wanted a full cigarette, and it was then I realized that I was getting addicted to them. I didn't want to become a smoker so I told my husband that I couldn't light his cigarettes for him anymore. That was the end of my experimenting. In truth, I realized that I'd much rather enjoy a milkshake or an ice cream cone than try to mimic someone else's idea of what is sophisticated, glamorous, or cool.

I don't recall any of us young people doing things out of a desire to be bad. I think the things we did were more because the temptation looked exciting or else we did it on a dare. I think the crowd you pick and the friends you run with are a reflection of your desire to be good. For the most part, I had a good group of friends, but that isn't to say that we didn't get into trouble sometimes. Luckily for me I was a well-loved child with a supportive mom and dad, no matter how I disappointed them sometimes.

After Mom and Dad moved to Nelson in May 1943, near the end of the school year, I managed to pass grade eleven. This was my first whole summer in Nelson and it was mostly spent at Lakeside Park beach. Mom wanted me to attend the Christian Science Sunday school in downtown Nelson. She had not taught Ray and me the rudiments of religion when we were growing up, and I followed along after my friends, mostly in the Trinity United Church style, or at least the Protestant way, due to our Protestant Irish background. I understand now a lot more about how friends influence a person and how to choose them for a good influence. But I did have a particularly good friend, Elaine Hughes, a pal from the Christian Science Sunday school, on whom I was a particularly bad influence.

We were in grade eleven, and the two of us loved to skate. One day, I suggested we take the afternoon off from school and go to the skating rink. She agreed. We snuck our skates out, but we forgot two very important elements. One was we were skipping out of the principal's Latin class, and the other was that my dad used to take walks on his day off to visit the rink to see who was skating. I guess this double set of events showed we were not hardcore school skippers, or truants, as they were called, or we would have thought it out better and got away with it.

Yes, my dad did come to the rink that day; we knew our goose was cooked when I looked up from the rink ice to see him watching me. Yes, we were caught and tried and found guilty. When I had reached home, Dad was already there. Mom asked me, "Shirley, did you skip school today?" What was I to say, when the witness to our crime beat me home? Needless to say, that was the end of our truancy career.

At school the next day, Elaine confessed first. Mr. Rogers met us on the stairs opposite his office. He greeted us with, "Well, girls, how was skating yesterday?" Elaine's mouth fell open in astonishment, and she gasped, "How did you know?" Obviously, the churches all taught the quality of honesty. He answered, "I didn't, but I do now. Two days' detention, and you will be doing Latin." Ugh! I think he even supervised us.

Mr. Rogers was an Anglican. A plaque honouring him was placed in St. Saviour Pro-Cathedral, in Nelson, for him. His name is commemorated in one of the church's beautiful stained-glass windows. Maybe the most important lesson that Mr. Rogers taught me was that not all male teachers are bad. To me, and to any other student who knew him, Mr. Rogers was wise, kind, and patient. He was interested in the Spanish language, probably because of the Latin he taught. I also was interested in that language, and he offered to help me, but I did not do much with it at the time. The desire to learn Spanish and to really master it to the degree I would like has finally borne fruit after all these years—at least, Mr. Google and I can write it, somewhat. I was always glad I had studied Latin when I realized it was the basis of all the Romantic languages and also a big contributor to English.

My first Christmas in Nelson, in 1943, was a bit of a shock to me. It was Christmas, but there was no snow on the ground! I had heard about "green Christmases" with no snow, but to me it was inconceivable, after living in the snow-laden mountains. I remember Dad going up the Ymir road to cut us a Christmas tree. At least the tree meant it was Christmas, even if there was no snow.

Aunt Grace, Mom's sister, had come to visit us from Saskatchewan that Christmas. Mom was one of four sisters. The youngest sister, Marjorie Alys, had passed away when she was only seventeen, and the other two sisters still lived in the Prairies, Aunt Grace in Saskatchewan and Aunt Edna in Manitoba, where our grandparents were from. Aunt Grace liked the British Columbia mountains, but not Aunt Edna. I think they cut off her vision and made her feel closed in. Also, our mountain roads, with their sharp corners, were somewhat frightening.

While Aunt Grace was visiting, she and Mom went shopping. Whenever Mom wanted to go shopping for a new dress, she had a favourite saying: "Well, I need something different, as everyone is beginning to recognize me by what I am wearing," meaning she was wearing the same dress so many times that her friends knew her by what she was wearing before they even caught up to her. She did not like it when she met someone wearing the same clothes as herself, either. She said it was like meeting yourself on the street, and sometimes when standing next to the other lady she did not look so good!

When Aunt Grace had asked me what I would like for Christmas. I said I would like a little lamp for my bedroom. Instead, her gift to me was a lovely pendant with a "Pan," a funny little creature, half man, half goat, with goat legs, ears and little horns, sitting and playing a pipe-like flute. The pendant was made by the Wedgwood China Company. I still wear it sometimes.

I wondered where Ray was and what kind of Christmas he was having. In addition to it being my very first green Christmas, it was also my first one without Ray. After Ray was called up, he spent about five months training in Canada, first in Vernon, BC, and then in Calgary. Mom, Dad, and I went to visit him in Sicamous in April 1943, just before he was to head to Halifax for embarkation to Great Britain. It was our last visit together. A letter and photo from him informed us that when he arrived in London, he had the opportunity to join with the Seaforth Highlanders Regiment of Canada, 1st Canadian Infantry Division, as our dad had done in the First World War. After he received his new unit identification and assignment, he was immediately sent to North Africa with his new regiment to continue training.

Ray's early letters stated that mostly they were training and waiting for the push up into Italy. While in North Africa, Ray wrote that he got some kind of irritation, which he described as desert sores all over his face and neck, and that he was all bandaged up. Some kind of ointment that they made using parts from the corkwood trees was applied to the sores. He wrote, "I have a slit for my eyes and a small hole for my mouth, and boy, are they itchy. It is all I can do to keep my hands off them." This was in Ray's letter dated April 29, 1943.

Ray was very good about writing home. Mom and Dad sent him parcels, but they took months to catch up to him. He wanted a picture of me to show his buddies, so one of my friends took one of me in a bathing suit at Lakeside Park to send to him. The photo was among his belongings that came home to us later that year.

When we finally got Ray's Christmas card dated November 17, 1943, it was sometime after New Year of 1944, so we had some reason to believe he was still stationed in North Africa. Little did we know he had already been sent into Italy; I believe this was his last correspondence to us.

In April 1943, his regiment, the Seaforth Highlanders of Canada, were assembled in North Africa under the operational command of the 1st Canadian Infantry Division. They moved into Sicily on July 10 as part of Operation Husky, then crossed into Italy on September 4. Including their first engagement with the enemy in Sicily, to the end of December 1943, they won ten major battles and many smaller ones. By the end of December, however, they had lost large numbers in the bloody battle of Ortona. Ortona was where Ray had spend his Christmas. After this battle, the Seaforth Highlanders of Canada were pulled back from the front line to rest and wait

Ray wearing his new Seaforth Highlanders of Canada Glengarry cap with metal regimental cap badge. Photo taken overseas; Mom received it August 5, 1943.

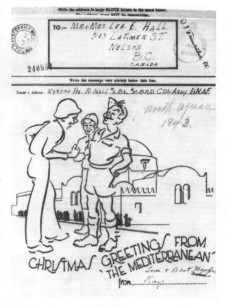

The author in a bathing suit, ca. spring of 1944.

Christmas card from Ray, sent November 17, 1943.

for the integration of new reserves before being called upon to break the Hitler Line. Ray was killed in action on May 23, 1944, in the Liri Valley, in the battle that broke the Hitler Line. It was one of the most intense battles of the Italian Campaign and was won by our troops at a great cost.

Brother Ray lost his life at age twenty-one. His remains are buried in the Canadian War Cemetery at Cassino, in the Lazio region of Italy.

ONE OF THE after-school groups I attended was the Trinity United Church young people's group. It was led by a very active lady named Mrs. Elva Kettlewell. She was a rather short person who was full of love for her Sunday school class and our young people's group. Sometimes the St. Paul's young people's group, on Stanley Street, would join in our activities, but Mrs. Kettlewell seemed to be able to handle us all. I'm embarrassed to admit that the socializing was a large part of what drew me to Sunday school throughout my high school years. It wasn't until later, when I was in my early twenties and I had my own children, that I felt I learned how to really pray.

Our fun times included going out to Camp Koolaree over the weekends, where we slept in the lodge and ate at the cookhouse. The summer camp was run by the United Church, so we would have our Sunday school

Ray Hall, Christmas 1943, Ortona, Italy.
FROM UNIDENTIFIED NEWSPAPER

mornings at the outdoor chapel. Camp Koolaree was about eight miles east of Nelson, on the south shore of the West Arm of Kootenay Lake. To get there, we would take the Nelson and Fort Sheppard train and be dropped off on the tracks near the camp, then walk the rest of the way to the lake. Mrs. Kettlewell surprised me one day while I was in the cookhouse. She asked me if I was related to a Tom Hall who had been one of the cooks at the camp. I told her he was my grandfather. That was the first time I knew Grandpa Hall had still been cooking after their retirement and move to Nelson.

At Koolaree, everyone usually had a great time. We would hang out with friends and go hiking, canoeing, swimming, and diving off the float into the lake. However, there is one particular weekend at the camp that was the start to one of the worst weeks of my young life. It was the weekend before Tuesday, May 23, 1944.

On Friday, the start of this particular weekend, the United Church young people's group and our fearless leader, Mrs. Kettlewell, took the last train of the night out of Nelson to travel east as far as Koolaree. The weather was great, although the water was yet too cold for swimming, but we had other things to do. On Sunday, we had our own church service. Bruce Arneson, a member of our group, gave the sermon. The chapel in the woods was

The Trinity United Church young people's group, 1944,
Nelson. The author is seated at the top left.

dappled by the sun shining through the trees. That afternoon, a few of us were sitting on the diving board on the float, enjoying the sunshine. There were five or six of us, and each of us sat leaning against the bent knees of another kid; we often liked to sit this way. I had been leaning against Alex Freeman's knees. Someone at the back of our chain of sitters lost their balance, and our house of cards began to collapse, with dire consequences for myself. As I sat up to avoid falling off the diving board, Alex lost his balance, his feet flew up and his hobnailed boots came crashing together, gripping my head firmly between them. Then, while Alex was regaining his balance, his feet pulled me backwards on the diving board by my head, at which point I lost my grip. The only thing that kept me from completely falling

The United Church young people's group at Camp Koolaree, enjoying the sunshine on the dock on a Sunday afternoon in May 1944: *L–R*: Bob Emory, Les Rogers, Ron Lyons, Jack Steel, in front of Mrs. Kettlewell (in hat), the author peeking over her left shoulder, Margaret and Bev McCosham in front of pole.

was the fact that he still had my head caught firmly between his boots. I don't remember much after that. There was no blood, but I'm sure some first aid was applied by Mrs. K. I had a very bad headache and started to worry how I was going to walk the eight miles of railroad back to Nelson and the other mile up the hill to home with all my gear the next day.

I have very little memory of that Monday walk home from Camp Koolaree. I remember carrying all my own gear home and focusing on the railroad ties—one short step, one step long, just like walking with Uncle Wat. By the time I reached home, Mom took one look at me and put me to bed in their room, and then she sat down and prayed. I don't believe

Nelson High graduating senior class
of 1943-44. The girls outnumbered the boys.

anyone, either at camp or on the walk home, felt that this accident was more serious than what appeared to be just a knock on the head.

By Wednesday, May 24, I was a bit better but still in bed. That afternoon, there was a knock at our door. Dad was home, so he answered it. It was the telegraph boy. He handed Dad a telegram and had him sign for it, and then the boy continued on along our block past two more homes to deliver another telegram to Mrs. Wilson, Jack Wilson's mom. He had possibly already delivered a telegram to the Leigh McBride home, just around the corner from us on Stanley Street. Major McBride had been wounded in the same battle in which both twenty-one-year-olds, Jack and Ray, were killed.

The telegram began with the standard wording that every parent prays they will never receive: "We regret to inform you..." At first, when you get such a letter, you feel sad, or angry with God, or both, for not answering your prayers to keep your child or sibling safe, seldom remembering that the enemy had a family, too. But God did answer Mom's prayers for me. I started to regain consciousness, and my memory began to come back. I was back in school the following Monday, with my head still intact, but my heart sick at the loss of my only sibling.

When the war had ended, one of Ray's buddies came to visit us at our home. I could not face him, so I took off to the skating rink. I have always regretted doing that. Mom and Dad were very grateful for his

Signatures of Nelson High graduating
senior class of 1943–44.

thoughtfulness, especially because he was not a local boy. I suppose the soldiers who were good friends had planned it that way: to talk to each other's parents if the others did not come home again. I did not have the courage, though, to hear what his friend might say. Dad was a returned solider from the First World War, so he understood how important it was to have this visit.

I remembered back when war was being considered by the powers that be, and one day some of us children were sitting on the school steps discussing, to the best of our ability and knowledge, what war was. Of course, we had no real understanding of what it was. This was when we were still in Sheep Creek. I guess the word to describe what we felt would be "excitement," with all the war recruitment and patriotic posters and radio broadcasts. But Mr. Unsworth was right, war would not be fun. Most of our parents knew what it was about, too, because they had already experienced the effects of a world war in their time. Little did we know that some of these boys would lose their lives in this upcoming war.

FAY HOUSE AND I were best buds. In fact, our joint nickname was "House and Hall." Her dad was a Nelson city constable. Every Saturday night a public dance was held at the Eagles Hall with a live orchestra. It was the days of the jitter-bug style of dancing. I had learned most of the moves as a kid in Sheep Creek from some of the older girls, so I wasn't too bad at it, but jitter-bugging was not my favourite style of dancing.

My folks let me attend the dances, but Fay's dad did not, even though we both loved to dance. So, I went alone. Constable House showed up in his uniform at least once to check up on the situation. I went to a couple of dances, but it was not fun going alone, so I decided I'd rather go skating instead. Fay and I did happily attend the school dances, because we at least could always have each other for a dance partner.

The same orchestra that played for the public dances often played for our school dances, which were different than our school mixers. We had formal dances about once a month. The dances started at 8:00 p.m., and students would usually go with a date. It was a good way for us girls to get to know the older boys, as we were getting a little short on senior boys because of the war. Some of the dances were attended by British or Australian pilots staying in Lethbridge, Alberta, for flight training. Families in Nelson invited the pilots on their leaves from the base in Lethbridge to be their house guests. The boys were young, cute, and well behaved. I personally never knew of any bad or inappropriate behaviour on their part. One of the airmen, named Ken, sent me a picture of him and his mates Geoff and Frank, taken sometime later, in their flight uniforms while they were still training on the Prairies.

The school had a lot of mixers, which were dances where we mixed socially with the other classes. These dances took place on Friday afternoons, but we were not required to attend. Sometimes, we would have school musicians playing, but most of the time the music was canned, meaning that we played records. Each grade took turns as host for the dance.

Nelson High also had a drama club, which I joined and enjoyed. One year, we put on a play in the Capitol Theatre, though I don't remember what it was about. Other ways we spent our time when not in school was doing anything we could do to help with the war effort. Being involved with groups and activities that supported the war encouraged each other to remain positive and helped many of us endure the loss of someone close. Without a word, people understood the grief you felt, and focusing on helping to make someone else's soldier more comfortable with the hopes of bringing them home safely made the sorrow a little easier to bear. Some of our war-drive activities included volunteering for the Junior and Senior Red Cross, by selling war saving stamps (all our extra pocket money went there) and collecting cancelled stamps, salvage paper, old clothes, silk hosiery, fat, glass, rubber, scrap metal, and so on, as well as marching on the Civic Centre parade ground and participating in "tag" days. War saving stamps provided an affordable way for people, especially kids, to contribute their money. It was a program to loan your money to the government to help pay for the war. A person would buy special government printed stamps at twenty-five cents per stamp and affix them to a stamp card. When the stamp card was filled with four dollars' worth of stamps, the card was redeemed at the post office or mailed to the War Savings Committee and a five-dollar war savings certificate was issued, registered in the name of the card holder. The stamp images varied so they were interesting to collect and could be bought from the post office or almost any retail store with one's spare change. The money raised by the saving certificates was used by the military to purchase more artillery, planes, tanks, and supplies for the soldiers. The war saving certificate could be redeemed by the registered holder seven and a half years later at the full maturity value of five dollars, or earlier for a lesser value. Tag days were another way to raise money. On special days during the month, and on holidays like Easter and Christmas, the Red Cross would sell people a printed paper tag to wear that publicly showed you supported the war. The girls also participated in Victory knitting and sewing groups. The Red Cross provided knitting and sewing instruction booklets that explained the types of items service men and women needed and specific instructions on how to make them.

A poem in our Nelson High 1943 yearbook, *The Mountaineer*, illustrated how the war was also affecting our wardrobes. The tight, prim cardigans now moved over to make room for "sloppy joes," oversized sweaters or cardigans, or a boyfriend's oversized button-down shirt:

Co-ed of '43

She wears a long and sloppy joe,
She dotes on heavenly goo.
Her skirt is knee high to a duck,
Come on now gang, guess who?

She clanks and clonks with jewelry,
Her hair's a dizzy whirl,
Her shoes hang half way off her feet,
Her elbows are a whirl.

Boy's jackets that are a mile too big
Are now her latest fad
She just broke up with a smaller guy,
For a tall, broad shouldered lad.

This gal is really on the beam,
She doesn't miss a step,
She breaks, she shags, she rumbas,
In short, she's plenty hep.

Beneath her happy giddity,
Her heart's as true as blue,
Of course you've guessed who she must be,
She's Co-ed '43

Another poem of unknown authorship paid homage to our plight:

Farewell to silk hosiery
Farewell, dear silk and fond goodbye
Your other uses now we see
As parachute you'll land some guy
That's more than you ever did for me.

OUR GREATEST SORROW at this time was, of course, the loss of family members and friends. Although Jack Wilson's home was at the end of our block, I had not been aware that he was also in Europe, as Ray had not mentioned him in his letters until almost the end. As I mentioned earlier, Jack also lost his life in the war. Ray also mentioned Leigh McBride, Ray's army captain, and his brother, Ken, who had both lived just around the corner from us on Stanley Street. Ken, a captain in the Seaforth Highlanders of Canada, lost his life in Coriano, Italy, on September 16, 1944, but luckily his brother Leigh would make it back home. It seemed like everyone's family had someone deployed.

I used to pray every night for Ray to come home, whole and well, but maybe "Please God!" was not enough? I'm afraid I really did not know how to pray, and I never asked, despite my faithful attendance at Sunday school; something more was needed—probably faith! Later in life, I understood that prayer was not about asking so much as it was knowing that God was really present and doing the job.

Every day, we would hang on every word of the radio newscasts to hear what was happening in England and in the rest of Europe. We read newspapers and magazines to glean any information we could as to when this war would be over. There was a magazine at that time called *Liberty*. A photograph in one issue featured some Canadian soldiers standing in front of a billboard, laughing and reading what was on it, which was an advertisement for tourism: "See Naples and Die." Apparently that was a well-known saying in Italy, and it meant that once you indulged in the magnificence and beauty of Naples there was nothing else you needed to live for. The photo did not name the boys in the picture, but, as often happened in photos, the tallest boy in it was my brother! Ray always did have an easygoing sense of humour.

WE YOUNG PEOPLE were all growing up so fast. That summer, after graduating from grade twelve, I even decided to venture to the other side of the service counter at the local soda shop and wait on people instead of being waited on. Fay and I still mostly window-shopped, but now that I was getting older, my allowance did not stretch far enough. Mom said, "You are old enough to work, so why don't you get yourself a job?" Hey, great idea, I thought. I heard that Gelinas' were looking for a soda jerk for their place on Baker St. Gelinas' Recreations was a twenty-four-hour local hangout that had a soda fountain bar upstairs and billiards and a bowling alley downstairs. That shouldn't be a hard job. So there I went, shy and scared, to ask a stranger for my real first job. And he actually said yes. My job, as a soda jerk, was to operate the soda fountain and learn the recipes and techniques to make special drinks, shakes, or ice cream desserts. It was a coveted position, kind of like the position of a coffee barista today.

My first day at the job did not go as smoothly as I would have hoped, though. My boss told me that Mary, a nice lady who already worked there, would show me how to make milkshakes and sundaes, and she did. Then she had me start waiting on customers. The first thing my customer wanted to know was what flavours there were. I had memorized the flavours list and proceeded to recite them all. For some reason, customers always seemed to pick the last one that I had rattled off. It took me a long time to figure that one out, until I had realized that I had rattled all the

Nelson High Senior Matrics class and returning
soldiers on Cominco Career Day in Trail, ca. 1945–46.

flavours off so fast that they only really heard the last one. Once I figured
that out, things started to go more smoothly.

The other thing I was up against was that the older worker, who'd been
there for ten years or so, wanted to play her game on me, so she would
suggest I do something really stupid to see if I was smart enough to catch
on. I was a very trusting person, so of course I would not catch on before
it was too late. For example, just after midnight, during the third shift, it
was very quiet, and my co-worker said that she could handle the business
on her own and suggested I take off for the movies and then come back
to work. Without much more than a passing doubt, I accepted her sug-
gestion, having no idea that this was unacceptable, this being my first job.
Whether my partner was testing me or just wanted to get me into trouble,
I never asked, but it was pure inexperience and stupidity on my part to do
as she suggested.

I guess Mary must have told the boss, because he invited me into his office the next evening and confronted me about it. I told him how it had happened, and he said, "Of course you know I cannot pay you for those two hours. That is not the way to act without my permission and on my time." I could see that. Why he trusted me and let me keep the job was probably due to his experiences with teenagers. He had at least two sons. Well, they say confession is good for the soul. I now look at this episode in my life with shame for my lack of understanding of, or innocence about, the business world. Another hard-learned lesson, not unlike my hard lesson after the skating incident—although with the skating experience, I was aware of what I was doing.

MAY 7, 1945, was an exciting day: it was the day the word came that the armistice was signed when the Germans officially surrendered to the allies, Europe, and North America. Everyone—well, almost everyone—headed for Baker Street, accompanied by shouts and back-slapping, horns honking, singing, and laughter. I joined them after I had given some thought to my only sibling, now gone forever. Mom and Dad preferred to sit quietly at home, listening to what was happening in Europe over the radio, while I joined friends in the celebration. Officially, Victory Day in Europe was May 8, 1945, when all the Germans were to cease fire, but we started celebrating the moment we heard the news of the treaty on the radio.

But the war was not truly over, because there was still Japan to deal with; we all know how that turned out. It was the first time the atomic bomb was used, and Japan was the target. It shocked the world. It was unbelievable, but it finally brought humanity to its senses.

We realized that sons and husbands, brothers and sisters, would never come home again. A lot were buried in Italy like my brother. That doorman at the Civic Theatre did come home, but he never spoke about his experiences for fifty years, except to mention friends he had made. When his children asked him what the war was like, he only had one answer: "It was hell!" But for now, it was jubilation time. The schoolboys who had left would come home men, while we had only begun to grow up; dads would come home to resume their roles, to begin their lives again after four or five years of separation. Our Senior Matrics class grew quickly when former students returned home. As young soldiers returned home, they were given the opportunity to go to university or college, so there were not enough openings for graduating high school seniors to enrol. The solution was to

House and Hall, celebrating the author's
eighteenth birthday, February 1945, in Nelson.
I was wearing Ray's retailored suit, and the handkerchief
that was a gift Ray had sent me from England in 1943.

offer a Senior Matrics class at Nelson High, an equivalent to the first year of
college. Nelson only offered the Senior Matrics class in 1945–46. Cominco,
the smelter in Trail, held a career day for our class to educate returning
soldiers about opportunities still before them.

THE KETTLE VALLEY Express ran a full passenger train daily between
Nelson and Vancouver. The full passenger service included a sleeping car.
I mention this because Mom and I had to take Dad to Vancouver for an
operation at the Shaughnessy Military Hospital, and he needed to be in
bed for the trip. Since Dad was a veteran, his doctor in Nelson made all
the arrangements for the trip and the operation.

L-R: Uncle Wat, Aunt Grace, and the author at the Silverton lookout over Slocan Lake and the Valhalla Mountain Range, ca. 1943. The peaks of the Valhallas are hidden by the low clouds. I was wearing the coat that I designed, which Aunt Grace had patterned and Mom had sewn for me.

Ray, easygoing and always with a smile. In army training in British Columbia, 1943.

It was about mid-February, just before my eighteenth birthday, when we boarded the train in Nelson and headed out to Vancouver. When we reached Farron Hill in the Monashee Mountains, a snowslide had come down in front of our train and another one at the back of it, boxing us in. I remember looking across a deep snowy ravine, like the one today on the way to Christina Lake on the Blueberry Paulson Pass, spanned by a bridge; pretty well all you could see was snow. We were there for some hours waiting for a plough to clear out the tracks, but no one seemed to be frightened. Fortunately, we had a dining car with the train (and a really cute porter). When we finally did get to Vancouver, we got Dad admitted to the hospital. Mom's brother, my Uncle Bert, had a small place in downtown Vancouver

Freddie Stainton, in a military photo sent home to his mother, 1944. He enlisted
July 21, 1942, served as a private in the Canadian Army, and returned home
February 9, 1946, "to return to civil life on demobilization" of his unit.

Last photo taken of Ray, aged twenty-one, wearing his Tam O'Shanter
with Seaforth Highlanders of Canada metal regimental cap badge. Italy, 1944.

at the time, so we were not alone; however, the hospital was some distance
away from where we were boarding, so we travelled back and forth to the
hospital by streetcar.

Mom was not fond of big cities. One day, she and I were walking downtown when she remarked, "What I don't like about big cities is that you
never see anyone you know." Just at that point I caught a glimpse of a
sailor on his way to his ship, carrying a duffle bag on his shoulder. (The
Asian-Pacific part of the war was still being fought at this time.) I walked
over to him to speak to him, with Mom hurrying behind me, asking me
what I was doing. I had recognized this sailor as Jimmy McDonough, one
of Ray's and my schoolmates and the brother of my good pal, Grace Louise
McDonough, from when we lived in Sheep Creek. I turned to Mom and
said, "There, Mom, you *do* know someone in Vancouver." We had neither
seen nor heard anything of him since we had moved to Nelson. Seeing
Jimmy there at that moment was one of the marvels of my life, but I never
heard news of him or the McDonough family again.

A few more days passed while Mom and I waited to see what the word
was on Dad's surgery, but I was missing school, so Mom decided to send

me back home on the train while she continued to wait with Dad. This was within days of my birthday. When I got back to Nelson, Fay House came to stay with me until Mom and Dad came home a few days later. Dad never did have that operation, as he got better on his own.

When Ray had turned eighteen, before he went into the army, Mom and Dad had bought him a nice pinstriped suit. Now, for my eighteenth birthday, they had the tailor remake the suit into a fashionable skirt and dress jacket for me. I loved that suit, it was my favourite one to wear, and I have never forgotten Mom and Dad's thoughtfulness that birthday.

ON NOVEMBER 11, 1995, the BC Ministry of Environment, Lands and Parks honoured my brother, Private Raymond E. Hall, in the British Columbia Commemorative Place Name and Remembrance Day List. The practice of commemorating BC war casualties through geographical names started in the early 1950s, when the government began its Remembrance Day Program. Each year since 1989, the province has released a Remembrance Day list of geographical features named to honour the province's service men and women who made the ultimate sacrifice for their country and died overseas in war.

In Valhalla Provincial Park, an unnamed creek that flows out of Valhalla Lake into Gwillim Creek (Goat Creek) was named Ray Hall Creek to commemorate my brother. The waters that flow out of Valhalla Lake and pass through Hall Creek into Gwillim Creek flow close by the Clough Ranch in Slocan that featured so much in our lives as both children and adults. The Valhalla mountain range had also been a favourite area of Ray's in which to explore, fish, and hike. Translated, Valhalla means "Hall of the Slain." In Norse mythology, it is a great hall where warriors slain bravely in battle are received in honour, glory, and happiness. It seems fitting to me that my fearless brother, my hero, be remembered in such a beautiful, majestic mountain range.

As for me, I finished the first year of college (Senior Matric) in Nelson and took a job at a café in Ainsworth, about ten miles south of Mirror Lake. Later that summer, I finally won myself a date with Freddie Stainton, that cute Civic Theatre doorman, now a returned handsome soldier, by giving him back too much change and serving him a slice of cherry pie that had a pit in it. We later married and had a family of our own. But that's another story.

The author on Lake Laberge with the dog-sled crew, 2012.

EPILOGUE

I T TOOK A few years, but in the end, Mom got her wish and I got a higher education, graduating from Mount Royal College in Calgary, with a degree in sociology. Despite the challenges of the war and the Depression, I had enjoyed a very happy, carefree, and somewhat adventurous childhood, which is probably why I took such an interest in the poor kids that seemed to struggle with theirs. Later in life, I would work for a halfway house and children's centre, trying to help ease the pain and mental suffering of runaway and abused children.

One of my wishes came true, too—well, sort of. I was able to take art classes and paint portraits, although it was not in Spain, nor was it under the tutelage of Senor De László, and I was never nearly as talented as the portrait painter that I so admired. But I did it, and still do enjoy creating portraits.

As I have gotten older, I have never lost my sense of adventure, so for one of my birthdays, I decided to fulfill one other wish I had always had. Since I was a little girl, I have always loved sledding and often thought it would be fun to go dog sledding. In the winter of 2012, I made a trip to Whitehorse to see my youngest daughter. She lives on the south edge of Lake Laberge, by a large lagoon that freezes solid in the winter and looks like a humungous flat plate; skiers, snowmobilers, and dog sledders like to make paths on it. This seemed like a good opportunity for me to try out dog sledding, as my daughter's neighbours said they would take me for a short ride on their sled with the huskies.

One Sunday afternoon, I got up my courage and, saying a quick prayer or two, bundled up in warm clothes until I was unrecognizable and climbed into the sled. I wore goggles to stop the snow flying from the dogs' feet into my eyes, a cap on my head, and a hood over that, and leather-and-rabbit-fur mittens, which my daughter made for me years before. I wore a heavy pair of padded boots, a thick parka, and a blanket to top it all off.

My musher, Sandrine, had a sled chained to a tree and four large huskies straining at the harnesses. She gave me a pillow for my back and put one under my knees, and then, with me holding tight to the rails of the sled, my musher stood at the back of the sled and released the chains. The straining, jumping dogs felt the slack, and they were off like a shot.

Well, you would have thought we were on the Yukon Quest race! It wasn't until we were on our way that I discovered that the dogs only knew French. My own understanding is limited to "oui" and "non." I also found out some of the reasons the lead dog was so important. First, she was the only dog that knew I was a "cheechako." (In northern Canada, that means a tenderfoot or newcomer.) And it is the lead dog's job to listen to the musher, obey all the musher's (French) commands, and keep the other dogs in line. I have the greatest respect for the lead dog, Lobo. She was the only one my musher was steadily in contact with, as she was the one listening for her master's voice. Lobo's partner was Tipiag. The dog in back, on the right, was a female. She was the young one of the bunch and was distracted by the snow. You could see her thinking, "Here is my chance to eat this nice clean snow. I'll grab a mouthful every chance I get." Her name was Bunny. Bunny's partner was named Lingo.

It was a lovely day. Sandrine's husband had followed us on a snowboard pulled by another husky, and the snowmobilers ahead were making paths for us. We had gone quite a way across the lagoon when we decided it was time to head back home. Our friend's house, where we had set out from, now looked like a dot on the landscape. The lead dog finally got all the other dogs turned around, even with distracted Bunny still trying to eat snow. But Bunny got her harness twisted in the other dogs' leads, making it difficult for her to run. My musher decided to take time to straighten out the harnesses.

Sandrine had a long rope leading from the back of the sled up to the dogs, and when she left the back to go up to the dogs, I had to hold on to this rope. She went back and forth two or three times, each time asking me to hold the rope, and each time I did— except for the last time, as I felt there was no need to do so. Big mistake! As soon as Sandrine untangled

Bunny, the team took off without her. She was pulled, lost her rope, and fell face forward into the snow.

So here I was, once again, on a runaway sleigh, only this time I was not seven. My musher ran after me, calling to the dogs in French while I firmly gripped the sleigh rails and yelled "Whoa, whoa!" when I should have been yelling, "Non, non!" Then I thought, "There is a higher intelligence that these dogs can hear," and instantly the team slowed to a standstill and waited for our musher to catch up to us. After Sandrine had checked everything out, we went back to find my daughter waiting for us with camera in hand; apparently I had travelled a good way on my own. It was only then that I discovered there was a set of brakes on the sleigh.

The whole adventure was great fun. At the youthful age of eighty-five, I had finally fulfilled my desire to go for a real dog-sled ride.

So would I go again? Just try and stop me!

I have come to the conclusion that writing this little book is a precious way of correcting my errors and readying myself for my future. It has shown me characteristics that still need correcting, and I had better not waste any more time in doing something about them. Everyone needs to write a book about themselves that is truthful. Oh, there are certain things that are unmentionable, but I will take them to my Lord because I see I need to do some more listening!

APPENDIX A
FAMILY TREE

Johnson Pre Canada
i. 1772, to Quebec, Canada from Pennsylvania, USA

Richard Johnson
b. 1803, Quebec, Canada

child 2 of 11

Mary Grace Johnson (Clough)
b. 1836, York, Yorkshire, England
i. 1842, Quebec
m. 1855, Perth Road, Kingston, ON
d. 1912, Orillia, Simcoe, ON

note: sister of Fredrick Clough

Ira Johnson
b. 1827, Quebec
d. 1905, Orillia, Simcoe, ON

John Dillon
b. 1820 (circa), Kilkenny County, Ireland
i. as a young boy, NY
d. 1906, Strathcona, AB

Sarah Dillon (Gordon)
b. 1819, Armagh, Ireland
i. 1849, New York City, NY
m. 1852, New York City, NY
d. 1898, Orillia, Simcoe, ON

child 5 of 11

Sidney H. Johnson
b. 1864, Perth Road, Kingston, Frontenac, ON
d. 1941, Alberta

child 3 of 4

Sarah L. Johnson (Dillon)
b. 1858, Uxbridge, ON
m. 1889, N. Orillia, Simcoe, ON
d. 1938, Alberta

child 11 of 11

Ada Irena Cora Clough (Johnson)
b. 1878, Hampshire Mills, N. Orillia, Simcoe, ON
m. 1904, Nelson, BC
d. 1956, New Denver, BC

Walter Clough
b. 1870, Perth Road, Kingston, ON
d. 1947, Nelson, BC

note: son of Fredrick Clough and Catherine Robertson Guthrie

child 1 of 11

Phylander Johnson
b. 1856, Perth Road, Loughborough, ON
d. 1934, Greenway, MN

child 2 of 4

Maggie *Eliza* Johnson (Dillon)
b. 1855, New York City, NY
m. 1882, N. Orillia, Simcoe, ON
d. 1939, Greenway, MN

child 2 of 2

Mary *Phyllis* L. Cooper (Clough)
b. 1907, New Denver, BC
m. 1926, Kamloops, BC
d. 1994, New Denver, BC

Tracy W. Cooper
b. 1899, Louisville, KY
d. 1988, Nelson, BC

children
1- **Glen W. Cooper**
2- **Innes Cooper**
3- **Fern Pickering (Cooper)**

b. Slocan City, BC

child 2 of 6

Maggie *Grace* Gordon Stratford (Johnson)
b. 1885, N. Orillia, Simcoe, ON
m. 1910, Greenway, MN
d. 1961, Saskatchewan

George F. Stratford
b. 1874, Ontario
d. 1944, Saskatchewan

children
1- **Marjorie Eloise Craig (Stratford)**
2- **Lester Floyd Stratford**

b. Prince Albert Sub-Districts 1-24, SK

child 4 of 6

Zella Letitia *Edna* Augusta Young (Johnson)
b. 1888, N. Orillia, Simcoe, ON
m. 1916, Greenway, MN
d. 1949, Greenway, MN

William J. Young
b. 1874, Ontario
d. 1972, Greenway, MN

children
1- **Joyce Oxnard (Young)**
2- **Lex Young**
3- **Opal Downton (Young)**
4- **Iris Storie (Young)**
5- **Keith Young**

b. Greenway, MN

child 3 of 6

Jennie Irena Hall (Johnson)
b. 1886, N. Orillia, Simcoe, ON
m. 1917, Alamo Siding, BC
d. 1978, Nelson, BC

child 2

Shirley Stainton (Hall)
b. 1927, Spooner, SK
m. Frederick W. Stainton of Trail, BC

Abraham L. Holgate
b. 1791, Roxborough, Philadelphia, PA
d. 1847, Van Buren, IA

Elizabeth Holgate (Jones)
b. 1796, Milford, New Haven, CT
m. 1818, Pittsburgh, Allegheny, PA
d. 1880, Seattle, King County, WA

Sarah Hall (Currie)
b. 1799, Sheet Harbour, NS
m. 1815, Halifax, NS
d. 1859, Pictou, NS

William Hall
b. 1793, Devonshire, England
i. 1815, Sheet Harbour, NS
d. 1866, Sheet Harbour, NS

child 6 of 9

child 7 of 11

Edmund Carr
b. 1824, Bucksport, Hancock, ME
d. 1886, Seattle, King County, WA

Olivia Carr (Holgate)
b. 1831, Trenton, Butler, OH
m. 1856, King County, WA
d. 1881, Seattle, King County, WA

Mary Margaret Hall (Gammon)
b. 1833, Halifax, NS
m. 1855, Halifax, NS
d. 1891, Petit-Rocher, Gloucester, NB

Thomas Hall
b. 1828, Sheet Harbour, NS
d. 1897, Petit-Rocher, Gloucester, NB

child 3 of 6

child 4 of 6

child 5 of 9

Ulrich Abraham Carr
b. 1861, Seattle, King County, WA
d. 1913, Seattle, King County, WA

Henrietta Anna May Eclipse Reid Carr (Clark)
b. 1860, Oregon
m. 1887, King County, WA
d. 1927, Seattle, King County, WA

Carrie Maria Hall (Carr)
b. 1864, Block House Fort Decatur (Seattle), WA
m. 1889, Vancouver, BC
d. 1941, Edmonds, Snohomish, WA

note: sister of Elizabeth Carr

Thomas Brenton Hall
b. 1864, Petit-Rocher, Gloucester, NB
d. 1940, Vancouver, BC

child 1 of 3

child 3 of 3

Lena *Mabella* Purney (Hall)
b. 1890, Vancouver, BC
m. 1910, Chase, BC
d. 1934, Nelson, BC

Alexander E. Purney
b. 1885, Shelburne, NS
d. 1936, Slocan City, BC

Hugh Douglas Hall
b. 1893, Vancouver, BC
d. 1989, San Francisco, CA

Bertha Holgate Hall (Anderson)
b. 1891, Seattle, WA
m. 1925, Vancouver, BC
d. 1980 (circa), WA

note: daughter of Elizabeth Carr and Matthew Anderson

children

1- **Carolin Nina Pierce (Purney)**
2- **Jean Elva Purney**

b. Arrowhead, BC

3- **Elvin Curtis Purney**
b. 1920, Slocan, BC
d. 1944 Brussels, Belgium
Pilot Officer, 550 (R.A.F.) Sqdn.
Royal Canadian Air Force

4- **Keith Purney**
5- **Harry Purney**
6- **Ruth Leah Purney**

b. Slocan, BC

children

1- **Elizabeth H. Hall**
2- **Hugh D. Hall**

b. Seattle, King County, WA

child 2 of 3

Edmund Lee Hall
b. 1892, Vancouver, BC
d. 1981, Nelson, BC

child 1

Raymond E. Hall
b. 1923, Spooner, SK
d. 1944, Cassino, Lazio, Italy
Private,
Seaforth Highlanders of Canada

10440 Brackenridge Rd. SW
March 17/79 Calgary
Alta

Mr J W Paterson
Cobble Hill
B.C.

Sir—

In answer to your letter of the first I
will try to give you what information I can
Hope you can read my writing as I am
getting quite shaky at eighty seven years.
Before the High Arrow Dam was built near
Castlegar and the town of Beaton on the
West arm of the Arrow Lakes was flodded
the old settlement of Camborne
was a gold town a few miles up Fish
Creek

Vince Lade who was the foreman where I
was the cook 1933 to 36 at the Meridian Mine
that the Eva mine was discovered by an
old prospector & a young lad, they sold it
for 15:000 the old fellow proceeded to drink
up his share, the young fellow went to
Southern California & bought a Orange
Grove, some of the Old timers heard from
him later.
The Eva & Meridian mines amalgamated
but being low grade ore and poor milking
practices soon shut down
Jim Lade (Supt) & his brother Vince left for
the Atlen Country

2

then in 1932 when a Vancouver Co. opened
the mine the Lade brothers returned as
manager and fore man again
They built a flotation mill and installed
a water power system. the ore body was
not as large as expected and low grade
so the mine was closed in 1936.
The Silver Dollar a Silver & Lead prope
up the hill above Camborne took out
some ore but soon closed down about 19.

Sandon B.C.
I first went to Sandon in 1913 to Cook
at the Surprise Mine Alt. 7.300 ft. the
mine worked until about 1920, they buil
a Concentrator at Rosebery, all ore and
supplies were moved by aerial tram fro
Cody. and was hauled by four horse
wagons to Sandon, and by CPR to
Rosebery
At that time there were quite a few
mines working around Sandon & Cody
The Noonday & Freddy Lee at Cody wh
the Noble five mine had a tramway at
Cody
From Sandon there were the Sovereign
Reco. the Slocan Star later to become
the Silversmith. by far the biggest

roducer in Sandon. The Eureka. Ruth
Hope. Wonderful. and Miller Creek.
The Ruth Hope built a concentrator just
above the town where I worked in the late
1920's till the depression closed the town
Sandon was quite a town at that time as
it needed a lot of miners as most mines used
hand drills & single jacks. (four lb hammers)
to drill holes for blasting, As Pneumatic
machines had not been perfected at
that time.
About three miles up the North Fork of
Carpenter Creek at Three Forks was the
Mc Alister mine, they had a shipping point
the large building you speak of down stream
from Three Forks.
Also the mine dump you see from Three Forks
was the monitor, owned by George Formby
a small lead, he made enough from it to
raise a large family.
Above the monitor toward Sandon was
the Black Colt, later called the Viola
Mac. Viola Mac Millan a prospector
from the east bought it and took a lot
ore out before it played out
One mine I have not seen mentioned was
the Rambler Caribou near Three Forks
it shipped quite a lot of ore in the early
days

4

The first mine to be staked near Sandon
was the Payne. Near the summit of Payne
mountain be Eli Carpenter; they took
out about six million worth of ore, when
the near surface ore gave out, they dropped
down the hill a drove a cross cut to
intersect the Vien, but it proved to have
little ore at that depth so was abanded

Clarence Cunningham an American
mining man from Alaska arrived in
Sandon about 1916 with an idea
It was that a few of the mines had run
out of ore a shut down, so he would
take a lease and bond on several mines.
When one struck ore it was to carry the
others until another one found ore
At Sandon it was the Sovereign, the
Wonderful and Miller Creek At Silverton
The Van Roi & the Hewit
Above Alamo siding a couple of miles
below Three Forks the Queen Bess and
Idaho Alamo which was a washout
The Queen Bess shipped over a million
dollars of Silver Lead & zinc to the Trail
smelter at Alamo siding also a nice
home where he finished his days
Today all is a pile of old lumber

he used to ride a saddle horse from one
mine to the next, a rangy Chesnut Rex
that would walk the roads an trails at
four miles an hour.
I worked for him for years at several of
his properties

Last fall I attended a meeting of the
Museum committee at Sandon and left
any photos I had with them
Eugen Peterson and his mother have
been the only permanent residents of
Sandon over the years. she passed away
a couple of years ago, he is still leasing
properties
There is a mine working the last couple
of years just above the old town, they are
using the old Silversmith Mill to
prossess their ore
Hope this will be of some use to you
sincerely
E Lee Hall

MAP SOURCES

Arrow, Slocan, and Kootenay Lake Districts travel routes, ca. 1930, page viii

Compiled by Kristi Kirkelie from hand-drawn map by Shirley (Hall) Stainton
  and other period maps

Detail of *Perry's* mining map, page 8

O'Farrell, T.P. *Perry's Mining Map of the Southern District, West Kootenay.*
  Nelson: C.E. Perry & Co. Civil and Mining Engineers, 1893. *David Rumsey*
  Map Collection. davidrumsey.com.

Camborne townsite sketch, ca. 1934, page 84

Compiled by Kristi Kirkelie from the following:

*   "Camborne as I remembered in 1934–1997 by Edna Brigadie Daney,"
    Arrow Lakes Historical Society
*   annotations, corrections by Shirley (Hall) Stainton
*   Camborne town plat map, Lardeau Mining divisions BC, July 1902, from
    Milton Parent, *Circle of Silver*, p. 63
*   Land and Title Survey of BC, *ParcelMap BC*, "Camborne," pub.ltsa.ca/pmsspub
*   Archival photos from Arrow Lakes Historical Society and BC Archives

Sheep Creek townsite sketch, page 114

Compiled by Kristi Kirkelie from the following:

*   hand-drawn map by Shirley (Hall) Stainton

- Sheep Creek Townsite, plan of subdivision of part of Lot 10004 G.I., Kootenay District, BC, prepared 1911, registered May 18, 1914, Regional District of Central Kootenay
- District Lot 10004, Collins Mineral Claim, Kootenay District G.I., Crown Grant no. 1813/284, Montie J. Morgan, registered July 6, 1911. a100.gov.bc.ca/pub/pls/gator/gator$queryforms.menu
- Sheep Creek Mining Camp, West Kootenay, BC, C.O. Senécal, O.E. Prud'homme, and H. Lefebvre, Canada Department of Mines Geological Survey Branch, 1909
- Worldwide Elevation Map Finder. elevation.maplogs.com
- Archival photos from Touchstone Nelson Museum of Art and History and Shirley (Hall) Stainton Archives

King County/Seattle
- *King County Atlas, 1907*. Seattle, Washington: Anderson Map Co., 1907.
- *King County Atlas, 1889*. N.p.
- Historical maps and township plats of King County, Washington Territory.
- 1856 map of Seattle, drawn by Lieutenant Commander Thomas Phelps of USS *Decatur*, enlarged and revised by Clarence Bagley, December 1930. HistoryLink.org.

REFERENCES

Books and Articles

Basque, Garnet. *West Kootenay: The Pioneer Years*. Victoria: Heritage House
  Publishing, 1990.

"Brigadier General F.W.E. Burnham." Museum of Vancouver H971.282.10.
  openmov.museumofvancouver.ca/object/history/h97128210.

Canada at War. "WWII." canadaatwar.ca.

Cooper, Phyllis (Clough). *My Dad*. Self-published, 2006.

Crooks, Sylvia. *Homefront & Battlefront: Nelson BC in World War II*.
  Vancouver: Granville Island Publishing, 2005.

Dorpat, Paul. *DorpatSherrardLomont*. "Seattle Now & Then." pauldorpat.com/
  seattle-now-then-archive.

Kidall, Bob. "How Magnolia Got Its Name." *Magnolia Historical Society*.
  Blog post. magnoliahistoricalsociety.org/blog/wp-content/uploads/
  2-Magnolia1.pdf.

Matthews, Major James S. *Early Vancouver*. Vol. 7: *Narrative of Pioneers
  of Vancouver Collected between 1931 and 1956*. Vancouver: City of
  Vancouver Archives, 2011 [1956].

Old Time Trains. trainweb.org/oldtimetrains/articles.html.

Parent, Milton. *Circle of Silver*. Centennial Series, Vol. 4. Arrow Lakes:
  Arrow Lakes Historical Society, 2001 (map on p. 63).

Parent, Milton. *Silent Shores and Sunken Ships*. Centennial Series, Vol. 3.
  Arrow Lakes: Arrow Lakes Historical Society, 1997.

Procter-Harrop Historical Book Committee. *Kootenay Outlet Reflections:
  A History of Procter, Sunshine Bay, Harrop, Longbeach, Balfour, Queens
  Bay*. 25th anniversary edition. Balfour: Balfour and District Business
  and Historical Association, 2013.

Prosch, Thomas W. "A Chronological History of Seattle from 1850 to 1897."
[1900, 1901] Seattle Public Library. cdm200301.cdmhost.com/cdm/ref/
collection/p15015coll6/id/1392.

Seaforth Highlanders of Canada. "Breaking the Hitler Line: May
23, 1944." June 12, 2014. seaforthhighlanders.ca/seaforthnews/
breaking-the-hitler-line-may-23rd-1944.

Slocan Valley Rail Trail. slocanvalleyrailtrail.ca.

Smith, Douglas N.W. "The Nakusp & Slocan Railway: Early Railway Days
in the Kootenays." *Canadian Rail*, no. 410 (May-June 1989): 81–88.

Touchstones Nelson: Museum of Art and History. *Sternwheelers of
Kootenay Lake*, 2009. touchstonesnelson.ca/exhibitions/
sternwheelers/en/boats/moyie.php.

Vancouver Historical Society. *The Story of Vancouver*, 2012. vancouver-
historical-society.ca.

Walking Tour of Nelson's Heritage Buildings. Nelson: Welwood &
Fraser, 2013. kootenay-lake.ca/lakeside/Nelson/heritage/
NelsonsHeritageBuildings.pdf.

Archives and Organizations

Arrow Lakes Historical Society. alhs-archives.com.

BC Commemorative Place Name and Remembrance Day List.

BC Geographical Names Information System. apps.gov.bc.ca/pub/bcgnws.

BC Government Access Tool for Online Retrieval (GATOR), Crown Lands Registry.
a100.gov.bc.ca/pub/pls/gator/gator$queryforms.menu.

BC Ministry of Energy, Mines and Petroleum Resources. www2.gov.bc.ca/gov/
content/governments/organizational-structure/ministries-organizations/
ministries/energy-mines-and-petroleum-resources.

BC Ministry of Environment and Climate Change Strategy (formerly BC Ministry
of Environment, Lands and Parks). www2.gov.bc.ca/gov/content/govern-
ments/organizational-structure/ministries-organizations/ministries/
environment-climate-change.

Canadian Medical Directory Archives.

Church of Jesus Christ Latter-day Saints. *Family Search.* familysearch.org.

City of Vancouver Archives. searcharchives.vancouver.ca.

Columbia Basin Institute of Regional History. basininstitute.org.

Frontier College. "Our History." frontiercollege.ca/About-Us/History.

King County Archives. kingcounty.gov/depts/records-licensing/archives.aspx.

Library and Archives of Canada. bac-lac.gc.ca.

MyHeritage. myheritage.com.

Royal BC Museum, BC Archives. royalbcmuseum.bc.ca/bc-archives.

Salmo Watershed Streamkeepers Society. streamkeepers.bc.ca.

Sandon Museum and Historical Society. sandonmuseum.ca.

Slocan Valley Historical Society.

The Nelson Electric Tramway Society. nelsonstreetcar.org.

Touchstones Nelson: Museum of Art and History. touchstonesnelson.ca.

U.S. Department of the Interior, Bureau of Land Management. blm.gov.

University of British Columbia Library. "BC Historical Newspapers." open.library.
    ubc.ca/collections/bcnewspapers.

Upper Canada Genealogy. uppercanadagenealogy.com.

Vancouver Public Library. "British Columbia City Directories." vpl.ca/
    digital-library/british-columbia-city-directories.

Washington State Archives—Digital Archives. digitalarchives.wa.gov.

Washington State Library. "Newspapers." sos.wa.gov/library/newspapers_wsl.aspx.

Washington State University Libraries Digital Collections. content.libraries.
    wsu.edu.

ACKNOWLEDGEMENTS

I AM MOST GRATEFUL to my oldest daughter, Truus Zelonka, and eldest granddaughter, Kristi Kirkelie, for all their encouragement, dedication, and time in taking these little stories and bits of family history and knitting them into a book for me. I very much enjoyed having them with me while revisiting my childhood homes and memories.

My granddaughter has been a blessing. Without her countless hours of preparing images, fact checking, and compiling and editing the manuscript, this book would not have been possible.

I would also like extend a heartfelt thank you to my cousin Innes Cooper, a historian and one-time resident of Slocan, for our numerous phone calls reminiscing about our childhood at the Clough Ranch and for his assistance in confirming dates and locations with his records.

A special thank you also to John Kitura, for encouraging me to continue writing and for bringing my manuscript to the attention of Heritage Publishing House; Kyle Kusch and Rosemarie Parent from the Arrow Lakes Historical Society; Jim Robertson from the Nelson Electric Tramway Society; and Joyce Johnson from the Slocan Historical Society, for their research assistance and generous provision of photographs.

My granddaughter would like to give a personal thank you to Lara Kordic and Lenore Hietkamp of Heritage House Publishing, with whom she had the pleasure to work, for their kind support, valuable input, and professional coordination throughout the process of preparing the manuscript and images for publication.

ABOUT THE AUTHOR

SHIRLEY D. STAINTON (née Hall) was born in February 1927 on a farm near Spooner, Saskatchewan. Shortly after her birth, her family relocated to the Slocan Valley in British Columbia. While growing up, Shirley lived in many mining communities throughout the region, many of which are ghost towns today. After the Second World War, Shirley married a returned soldier named Fred, and they went on to raise three children. They retired in Balfour, BC, close to their roots. Shirley lived there, in the house on the lake that Fred built for her, until her death in January 2018.